D0281504

Teeline

GOLD

Speed
Ladder

Meriel Bowers
Stephanie Hall

the

most

successful

shorthand

system

HEINEMANN
EDUCATIONAL

Heinemann Educational Publishers
Halley Court, Jordan Hill, Oxford OX2 8EJ
a division of Reed Educational & Professional Publishing Ltd

OXFORD MELBOURNE AUCKLAND
JOHANNESBURG BLANTYRE GABORONE
IBADAN PORTSMOUTH NH (USA) CHICAGO

© Text: Meriel Bowers and Stephanie Hall 1992
© Teeline outlines: Teeline Education Ltd 1992
First published 1992
99 11 10 9 8 7

A catalogue record for this book is available
from the British Library on request.

ISBN 0 435 45355 6

Typeset by Fakenham Photosetting Ltd, Fakenham, Norfolk
Printed and bound in Great Britain by Biddles Ltd, Guildford and King's Lynn

About the authors

Meriel Bowers is a highly experienced shorthand tutor. She was a
lecturer at Huddersfield Technical College where she was
shorthand co-ordinator and course tutor for RSA and FTC
Teachers' Diplomas. She has been a Chief Examiner for the RSA
and FTC Teachers' Diplomas in Teeline shorthand and a JEB
examiner. She is a well-known author of Teeline books and also
runs Heinemann's shorthand seminars.

Stephanie Hall started teaching in 1979. She has been at Sutton
Coldfield College of Further Education since 1987, where she
teaches Teeline shorthand, typewriting, word processing and
information technology. She has taught Teeline to evening classes,
YT and day-release students, as well as trainee teachers, and runs
many of Heinemann's shorthand seminars.

Contents

Introduction

This new book in the Teeline Gold series introduces a new concept: speed development above theory. The ultimate goal in learning shorthand is to be able to write outlines speedily without conscious thought, and this book aims to do just that – develop speed.

Subsidiary to this central aim, other important objectives are also considered.

The development of confidence in reading and transcribing your own notes is one. Reading from print and another's shorthand is always good practice but the real test is outline recognition without hesitation from your own notes.

Exercises and explanations consolidate theory already known, strengthen weak areas and introduce more advanced theory not dealt with in *The Course Book*. This will ensure a complete mastery of the system. Also offered are ideas and guidelines to extend vocabulary and develop concentration and quick thinking.

Explanations of word groupings ensure you understand the principles behind them. It cannot be stressed too strongly that the use of groupings, apart from the simple ones with which all readers of this book should be familiar, is very personal. Groupings should be experimented with, accepted or rejected, but never learnt by heart. The authors have given suggestions but it is for the individual to decide whether or not to make use of them. Some writers reach high speeds using very few groupings, but once the principles are understood there is tremendous personal scope in using the wide variety of word patterns available in forming groupings without attempting to memorise.

You should take pleasure in adapting the principles to fit your own needs and we hope the ideas given will form a basis for reference. It helps to think of the sounds involved in forming groups of speed patterns, eg

    all parts (of the) world   years (a)go   boar(d of) directors

We hope you will be encouraged to devise your own outlines for words and groupings but you should never try to learn long lists by heart or copy meaningless shapes without understanding. Groupings are used after Unit 3 which are not shown as examples but follow the given principles. Reading these should develop and stretch your thinking capacity. A few longer passages have been included to develop stamina, but this is primarily a speed book.

This book is also a 'first' in that words introduced in the theory part of each unit are underlined for emphasis in the practice passage; speed drives are included regularly and the dictation passages are themed.

As stated earlier the major aim in shorthand learning is the development of speed. This book caters for students with speeds of 50/60 wpm upwards and there is potential for high speed development. It should be remembered that it is quite common to be faced with a speed plateau at around 80 wpm, but once this has been overcome it takes roughly another 10 hours to progress to an extra 10 wpm.

Outlines given in this book may not always be written in the same way. This is sometimes done intentionally to show Teeline's flexibility. Neither may the outlines necessarily agree with the ones in *The Word List*, but again this stresses the wide diversity available within the framework of the rules.

It is not strictly necessary to work through the units in the order presented as each unit is capable of standing on its own. As by this time you will be innovative enough to deal with any theory anticipation found as a result of changing the set order, knowledge will still be developed and extended in an enjoyable way. Whichever approach is adopted this book is your key to confident, fast shorthand.

Acknowledgement

All the Teeline shorthand outlines in this book have been written by Stephanie Hall, to whom the publishers' thanks are due.

Unit 1
The Teeline philosophy

Success in Teeline depends on your attitude to the system and your ability to be flexible. As long as no basic rules are broken, an outline cannot be categorised as either 'right' or 'wrong'. Once you have grasped the basic principles, you can adapt outlines to fit in with your own particular style of writing. The Teeline outlines shown in this book are all safe and legible, but are not necessarily the only acceptable ones. You can use them or reject them – the choice is yours.

By now you will have adopted and developed your own individual style. Large handwriting produces large outlines and vice versa, straight-up handwriting is reflected in 'straight-up Teeline' and so on, but can even more be done to improve your outlines?

Are your outlines readable? Do you find them easy to write? Are you quite sure they will not be misread? If there is any shadow of doubt about these questions, now is the time to put things right.

Exercise 1.1
Writing Teeline

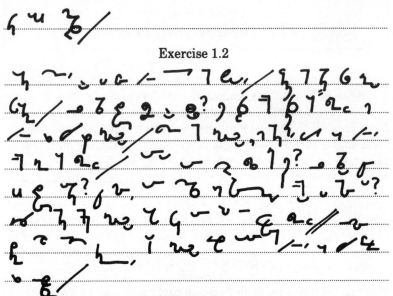

Exercise 1.2

Speed drive

Exercise 1.3 gives 40 words in Teeline. If you write them in half a minute, your speed will be 80 words a minute, but if you write them in 20 seconds, your speed will be 120 words a minute. Keep practising to improve your speed.

Exercise 1.3

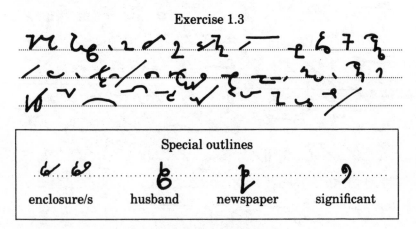

Special outlines			
enclosure/s	husband	newspaper	significant

Distinguishing outlines

personal   personnel

Practice sentences
Exercise 1.4

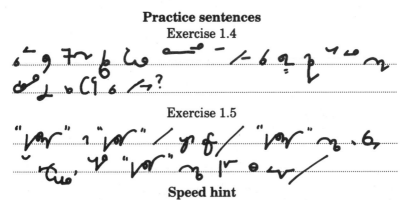

Exercise 1.5

Speed hint
Cultivate a light, flying style of writing Teeline with a minimum of wrist movement. Make sure you (and your notebook) are facing the desk squarely.

Dictation practice
Diamonds

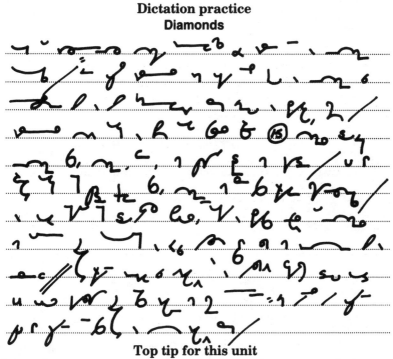

Top tip for this unit
Do not leave large spaces between outlines when writing Teeline. This wastes valuable time.

Unit 2
Getting a grip on word groupings

You have already learned and used word groupings and discovered for yourself that they reduce the outlines you have to write – and therefore increase your shorthand speed. It is not *essential* to use groupings, but your shorthand speed will improve considerably if you use as many as you possibly can.

OMISSION OF WORDS IN GROUPINGS

Groupings may be contracted by actually leaving words out in instances where it is obvious the words *must* be included in the transcription in order for it to make sense. Note that other letters may be omitted if it is safe to do so. Here are some suggestions. This is not a comprehensive list, though, as there are many other examples you could use. (See *Teeline Word Groupings* by George Hill and Meriel Bowers.)

And

this and that   here and there   odds and ends

up and down   years and years   near and far

for and against

Of/of the

most of all   rate of interest   in respect of

out of the ordinary   the fact of the matter   in the case of

To/to the

according to the   seems to have been   owing to the fact that

on the subject   with regard to   from beginning to end

A

for a long time   in a moment   quite a lot of

as a whole   times a day   as a result

Or

one or two   more or less   three or four

whether or not   something or other

Occasionally **R** is substituted for **or**:

this or that   sometime or other

men or women   somehow or other

If **or** follows **T**, it can be shown by writing **TR**:

right or wrong

Speed drives

Read the following sentences. Time yourself to see how long it takes, then time yourself again for a second reading and then a third one. When you are familiar with the sentences, practise them and then take them down from dictation.

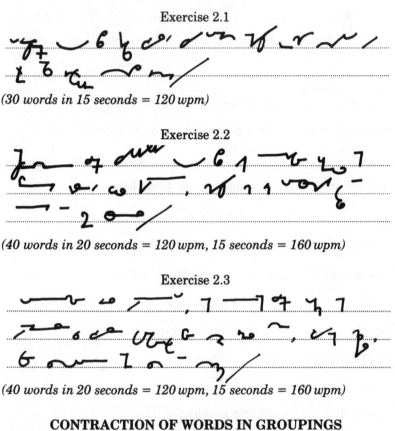

Exercise 2.1

(30 words in 15 seconds = 120 wpm)

Exercise 2.2

(40 words in 20 seconds = 120 wpm, 15 seconds = 160 wpm)

Exercise 2.3

(40 words in 20 seconds = 120 wpm, 15 seconds = 160 wpm)

CONTRACTION OF WORDS IN GROUPINGS

Some words may be shortened in groupings. You already know some of these, such as …… **poss** for **possible** and ……… **ite** for **committee**. Here are some more examples of these:

Possible

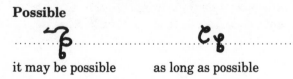

it may be possible   as long as possible

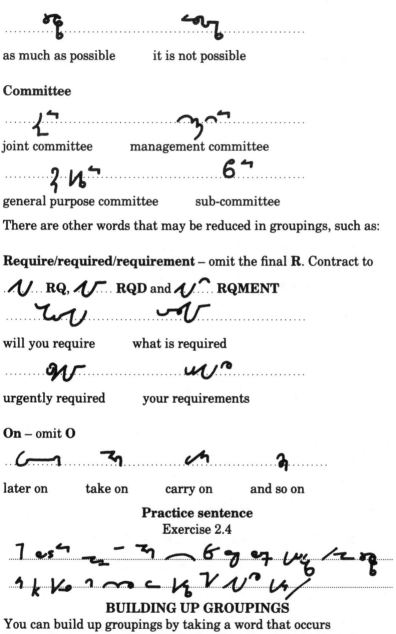

as much as possible   it is not possible

Committee

joint committee   management committee

general purpose committee   sub-committee

There are other words that may be reduced in groupings, such as:

Require/required/requirement – omit the final **R**. Contract to

RQ, **RQD** and **RQMENT**

will you require   what is required

urgently required   your requirements

On – omit **O**

later on   take on   carry on   and so on

Practice sentence
Exercise 2.4

BUILDING UP GROUPINGS

You can build up groupings by taking a word that occurs
frequently, such as **end**, and joining other words on to it, as in:

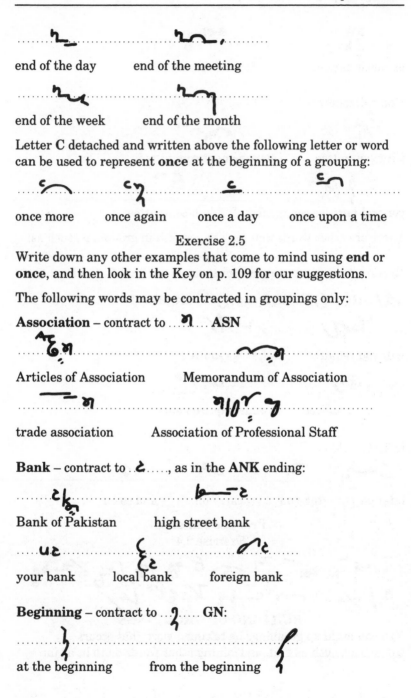

....
end of the day   end of the meeting

....
end of the week   end of the month

Letter C detached and written above the following letter or word can be used to represent **once** at the beginning of a grouping:

....

once more   once again   once a day   once upon a time

Exercise 2.5

Write down any other examples that come to mind using **end** or **once**, and then look in the Key on p. 109 for our suggestions.

The following words may be contracted in groupings only:

Association – contract to ....**٩**.... **ASN**

....

Articles of Association   Memorandum of Association

....

trade association   Association of Professional Staff

Bank – contract to .. **८** ....., as in the **ANK** ending:

....

Bank of Pakistan   high street bank

....

your bank   local bank   foreign bank

Beginning – contract to .. **٩**.... **GN**:

....

at the beginning   from the beginning

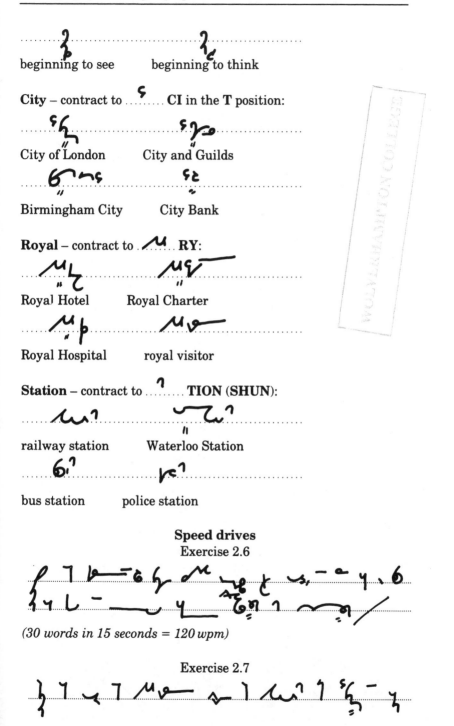

beginning to see   beginning to think

City – contract to .... CI in the T position:

City of London   City and Guilds

Birmingham City   City Bank

Royal – contract to ...... RY:

Royal Hotel   Royal Charter

Royal Hospital   royal visitor

Station – contract to .... TION (SHUN):

railway station   Waterloo Station

bus station   police station

Speed drives
Exercise 2.6

(30 words in 15 seconds = 120 wpm)

Exercise 2.7

(30 words in 15 seconds = 120 wpm)

Practice passage
Exercise 2.8
Memo to Secretarial Services Supervisor

Word grouping

I look forward

Speed hint
If a grouping comes quickly to mind when you are taking down dictation, use it; if not, write the outlines in full. Always read through your notes immediately after dictation and look through the passage for possible groupings. Practise these so that when the groupings are dictated again you will be more likely to remember them.

Dictation practice
Correspondence from Mark Rogers, who runs a company offering wedding services:

1 Letter from Wedding Services Ltd, replying to an enquiry

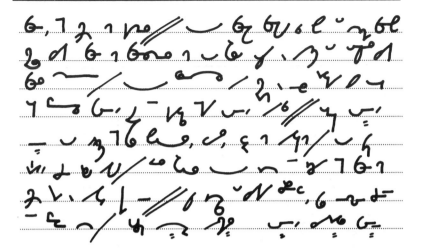

2 Letter to Mrs Harrison about the reception and flowers

3 Memo to the Cake Decorating Supervisor from Mark Rogers

4 Letter to Mrs Harrison confirming details

5 Letter to Mrs Harrison acknowledging settlement of account

Top tip for this unit

You can devise your own word groupings, particularly if your work involves specialist or technical terms and phrases. Form the grouping by contracting the words, then practise it until you have become familiar with it. Accurate transcription is very important, so always practise writing groupings several times before you actually use them. You will then be able to write them more quickly and transcribe the outlines correctly.

Unit 3
Contracting in groupings

Here are some more words that can safely be contracted *in groupings only*. Once again, remember that these are only suggestions – it is up to you to decide if they will be useful.

Authority

Use .... in **T** position and intersect preceding letter:

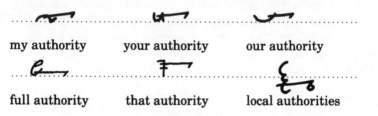

| my authority | your authority | our authority |

| full authority | that authority | local authorities |

Note: **Authority** standing alone is written in full (see Unit 11).

Be/been

In a grouping **be/been** may safely be reduced to the circle only:

to be .... or .... *instead of* ....

must be .... *instead of* ....

had been .... or .... *instead of* ....

should have been .... *instead of* ....

Try these out but remember that the full **B** may always be used if preferred. Remember to keep circle **B** larger than circle **S**.

Conclusion

Use .... and add circle **S** for the plural:

come to the conclusion   came to the conclusion

in conclusion   many conclusions

Enquiry/inquiry

Omit **RY**:

your enquiry   telephone enquiry   full enquiry   public enquiry

letter of enquiry   several enquiries   preliminary enquiries

Fact

Abbreviate to

as a matter of fact   it is (a) fact (that)

in view of the fact (that)   the fact (that)

Like

Contract to **K** ... **◟** ... in groupings such as:

I would like   I would like to say

I should like   I should like to say

I should like to say a few words

Opinion

Use ... **◝** ... *or* ... **◝** ... :

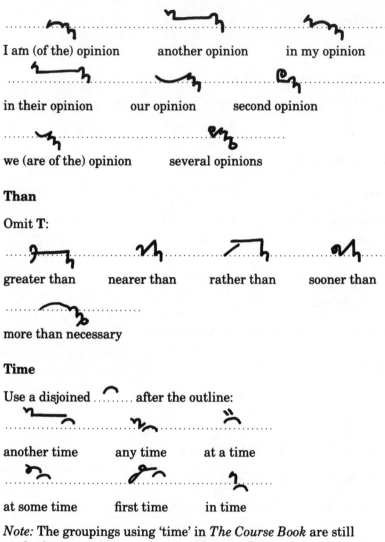

I am (of the) opinion   another opinion   in my opinion

in their opinion   our opinion   second opinion

we (are of the) opinion   several opinions

Than

Omit **T**:

greater than   nearer than   rather than   sooner than

more than necessary

Time

Use a disjoined ⌒ after the outline:

another time   any time   at a time

at some time   first time   in time

Note: The groupings using 'time' in *The Course Book* are still perfectly acceptable, so use them if you prefer.

Distinguishing outlines

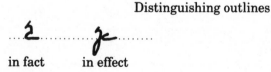

in fact   in effect

Speed drives
Exercise 3.1

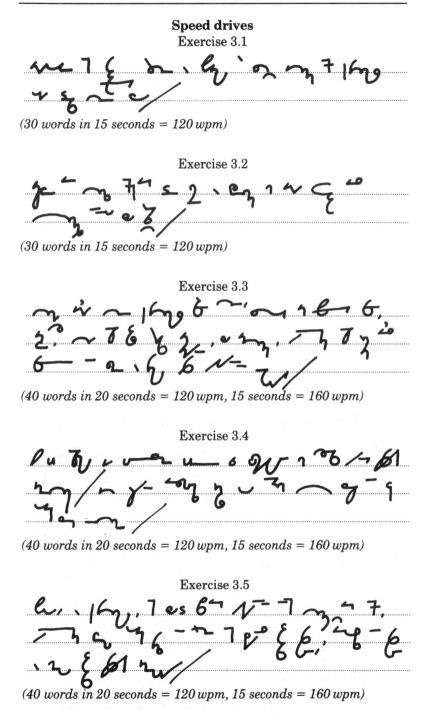

(30 words in 15 seconds = 120 wpm)

Exercise 3.2

(30 words in 15 seconds = 120 wpm)

Exercise 3.3

(40 words in 20 seconds = 120 wpm, 15 seconds = 160 wpm)

Exercise 3.4

(40 words in 20 seconds = 120 wpm, 15 seconds = 160 wpm)

Exercise 3.5

(40 words in 20 seconds = 120 wpm, 15 seconds = 160 wpm)

Speed hint

Keep your non-writing hand on your notebook to hold the pages
steady. Use this hand to turn over the page quickly by gradually
sliding the page upwards as the writing hand moves down it. When
the last line is reached, a quick 'flick' by the non-writing hand
turns over the page ready for you to start writing at the top of the
next page.

It also helps to bend over one of the bottom corners of the page
before a dictating session and this can be held as you slide the page
upwards. Do a big batch of 'corner bending' before you start your
dictation.

Dictation practice

Correspondence about a television set:

1

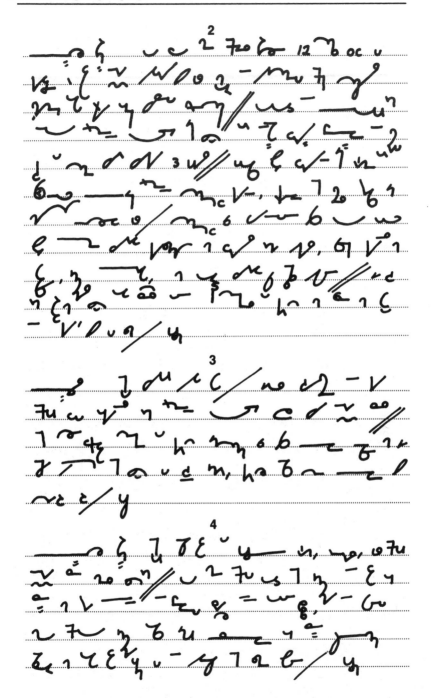

5

(Teeline shorthand outline)

6

(Teeline shorthand outline)

Top tip for this unit
Why not write your shopping lists in Teeline?

You could also write lists of television programmes you would like to watch and the words of favourite pop songs. Making a habit of translating everyday things into Teeline will help you build up your vocabulary.

Unit 4
T and D

T is *always* written *above* the writing line when standing alone, when preceded by **S** or a vowel only, or when it is the first letter in a word.

D is *always* written *on* the writing line when standing alone, when preceded by **S** or a vowel only, or when it is the first letter of a word.

Exercise 4.1

Can you read these words? The longhand is on p. 114 in the Key.

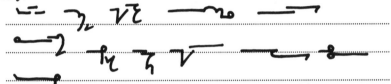

The following outlines differ only in the position of the **T** or **D**. Write the words in Teeline, then check them with the Key:

short/shared   retires/redress

WORD BEGINNINGS:
TRANS- and UNDER-

Remember that when words begin with **TRANS-** or **UNDER-** we omit the **N** for an easier outline. Read the following passage and practise the words before taking it down as dictation.

Practice passage
Exercise 4.2

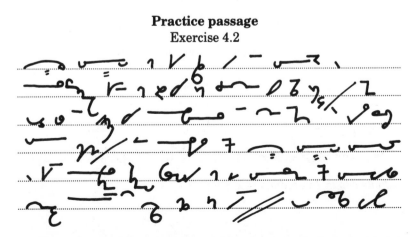

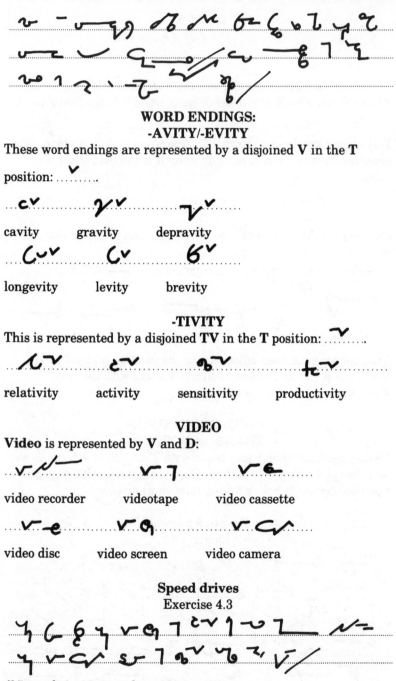

WORD ENDINGS:
-AVITY/-EVITY

These word endings are represented by a disjoined **V** in the **T**

position: ....

cavity   gravity   depravity

longevity   levity   brevity

-TIVITY

This is represented by a disjoined **TV** in the **T** position: ....

relativity   activity   sensitivity   productivity

VIDEO

Video is represented by **V** and **D**:

video recorder   videotape   video cassette

video disc   video screen   video camera

Speed drives
Exercise 4.3

(25 words in 15 seconds = 100 wpm)

Exercise 4.4

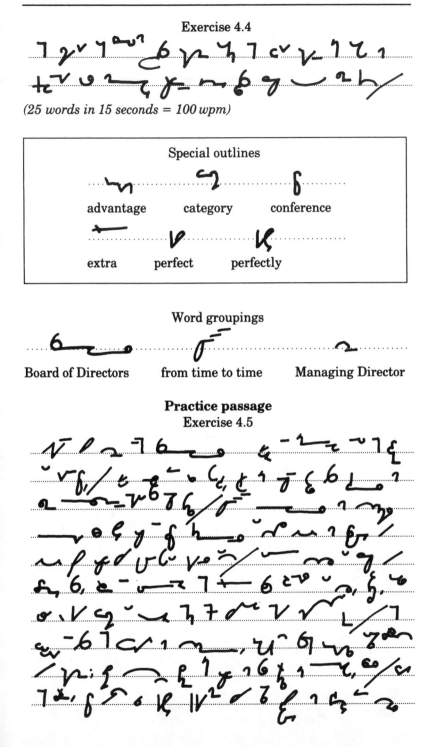

(25 words in 15 seconds = 100 wpm)

Special outlines

advantage	category	conference

extra	perfect	perfectly

Word groupings

Board of Directors	from time to time	Managing Director

Practice passage
Exercise 4.5

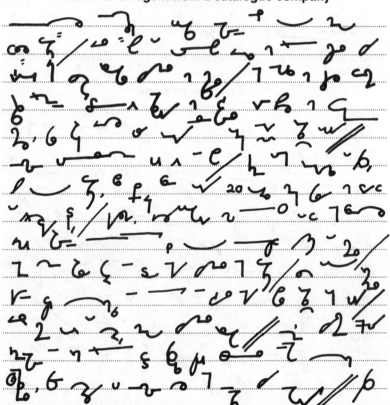

Speed hint

When you have finished taking down a passage of dictation, lift up the page of your notebook and see if there is an impression of your shorthand on the page underneath. If there is, it means that you are pressing too hard on the page when you write your outlines. This reduces your shorthand speed and may even make your hand ache. When you next take down dictation, try to concentrate on writing with a lighter touch – you should soon find that your shorthand speed improves.

Dictation practice

Correspondence from a gift and card catalogue company:

1 Letter to an agent from a catalogue company

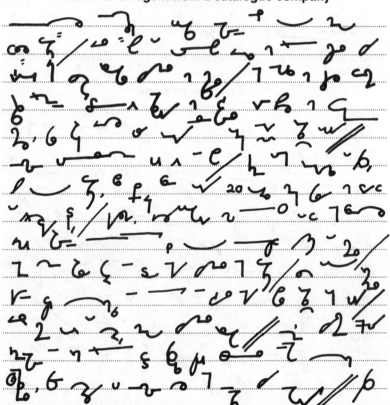

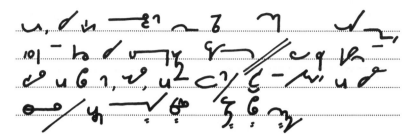

2 Memo from the Sales Director to the Stationery Manager

3 Letter to an agent about non-payment

4 Letter to an agent about giving up an agency because of ill health

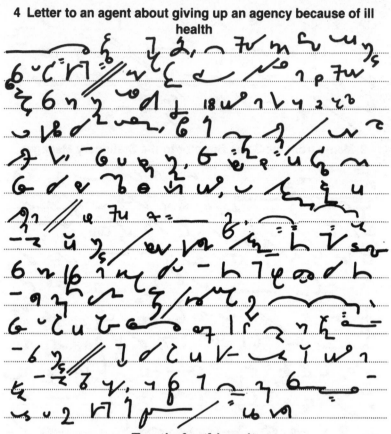

Top tip for this unit

Always use good writing materials. If you write Teeline with a
pen, make sure you choose one with a good flow of ink that does not
blotch. A fine ball point or a fibre-tipped pen is best as it enables
you to write small, neat outlines. If you prefer to write shorthand
with a pencil, make sure it is sharp – blunt pencils force the user to
draw large, thick outlines. Always have one or two spare pens or
pencils on your desk in case your pen runs out of ink or your pencil
needs sharpening.

Unit 5
Letter R

A REMINDER ABOUT R

What do we need to know about **R**?

1 It is always written *upwards*.

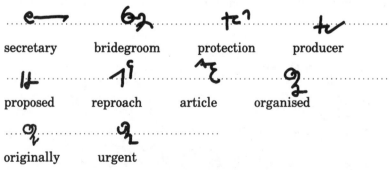

| girl | burn | first | garage | horse | rail |

2 It is always included in a word, either by writing the stroke as above, blending, writing up close to the previous letter, or intersecting. These all help when reading back.

| poster | dreamer | learner | market |

are examples of **R** blends.

3 It is sloped a little more than normal if followed by **G**, **P** or **Q** to enable these letters to cut the line:

| regular | rapid | request |

4 Stroke **R** is omitted, but implied, either by intersecting or close positioning when it immediately follows **B**, **C**, **G** and **P**. Vowels **A**, **O** and **U** are dealt with in a similar way by intersection, or tucking inside in the case of **U**:

| secretary | bridegroom | protection | producer |

| proposed | reproach | article | organised |

| originally | urgent |

5 We know instantly when reading back that if there is an intersection (or a close-up stroke) we must read **R** *immediately* after **B**, **C**, **G**, **P** or the vowel.

Speed drive
Exercise 5.1

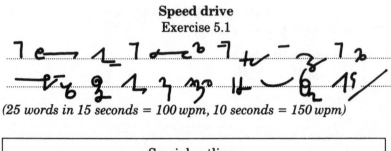

(25 words in 15 seconds = 100 wpm, 10 seconds = 150 wpm)

Special outlines

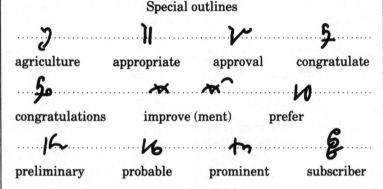

| agriculture | appropriate | approval | congratulate |

| congratulations | improve (ment) | prefer |

| preliminary | probable | prominent | subscriber |

Word groupings

| at the present time | shopping precinct | word processing |

Practice passage
Exercise 5.2

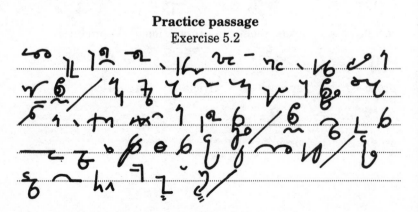

Speed drive
Exercise 5.3

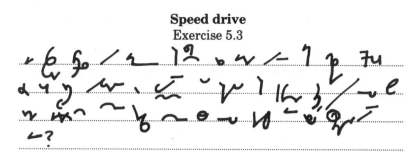

(50 words in 20 seconds = 150 wpm, 15 seconds = 200 wpm)

Speed hint

By leaving out the **R**, not only is there less to write, but it is a big help when transcribing. For instance, think about the word **order** which is written with one movement. Practise these:

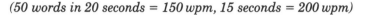

order   ordered   orders   orderly

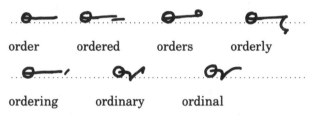

ordering   ordinary   ordinal

Dictation practice

Correspondence between the Green Finance Company and the Health Club:

1 Memo from the Manager, Pamela Green, to her staff

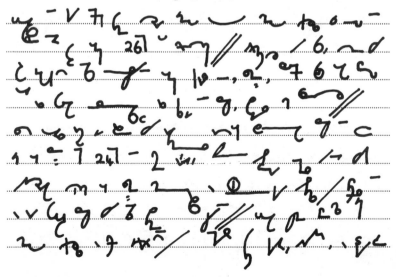

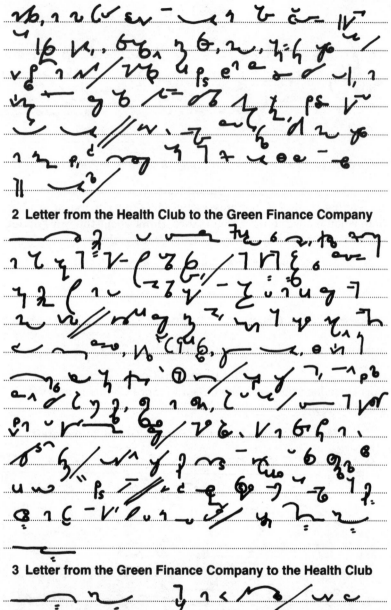

2 Letter from the Health Club to the Green Finance Company

3 Letter from the Green Finance Company to the Health Club

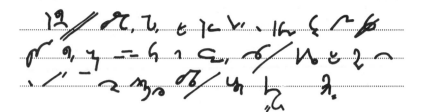

4 Letter to the Health Club from the Green Finance Company, enclosing cheque

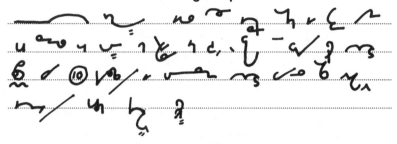

Top tip for this unit

If you are interrupted during transcription, quickly put a mark in your shorthand notebook at the point you have reached. When you return to the transcription, you will be able to find the correct place quickly.

Unit 6
Another look at vowels

Remember to keep vowel indicators small and concentrate on getting the correct angles when writing words that start with a vowel.

Exercise 6.1

Write the following words in Teeline, then check your answers with the Key on pp. 119.

accumulate   aversion   elaborate   identical   obligation   ultimate

You will recall that sometimes the full vowel is used:

A before R   array ✎ *now write:* area   arrears

E before P   epidemic ✎ *now write:* epilogue   episode

E before Q   equivalent ✎ *now write:* equate   equip

U before P   upon ✎ *now write:* upgrade   upright

Vowels may occasionally be written medially in a word to make a better outline, but either version may be used:

job ✎ *or* ✎   jacket ✎ *or* ✎
wage ✎ *or* ✎   banner ✎ *or* ✎

You already know that a full **A** is used for **AU** at the beginning of a word, as in **audience**: ✎. Also, words beginning **EV** have a disjoined vowel indicator above the **V**, as in **evaluate**: ✎.

Read the following sentence and practise the words before taking them down in timed dictation.

Speed drive
Exercise 6.2

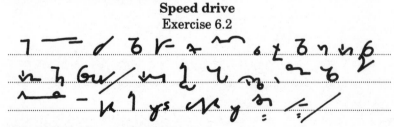

(40 words in 20 seconds = 120 wpm)

PREFIXES

In the Teeline Gold *Course Book* you have already met several prefixes. Here are some more that reduce the length of outlines.

AFTER-

A full **A** is used at the beginning of the word:

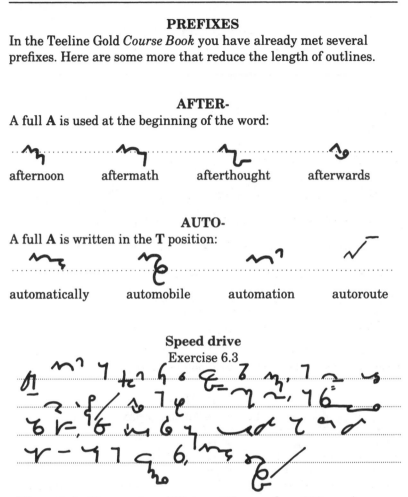

afternoon   aftermath   afterthought   afterwards

AUTO-

A full **A** is written in the **T** position:

automatically   automobile   automation   autoroute

Speed drive
Exercise 6.3

(50 words in 30 seconds = 100 wpm, 20 seconds = 150 wpm)

Reading passage

Test yourself on this passage. Time yourself to see how quickly you can read it and then read it again to see if you can do it in less time.

Exercise 6.4

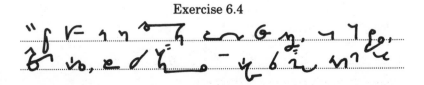

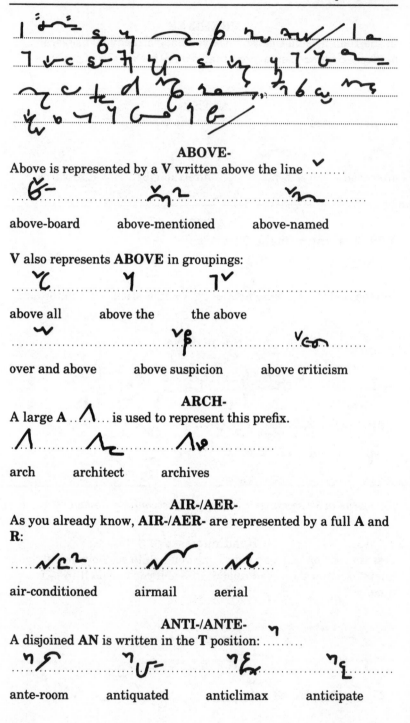

ABOVE-

Above is represented by a **V** written above the line ....

above-board   above-mentioned   above-named

V also represents **ABOVE** in groupings:

above all   above the   the above

over and above   above suspicion   above criticism

ARCH-

A large **A** ...∧... is used to represent this prefix.

arch   architect   archives

AIR-/AER-

As you already know, **AIR-/AER-** are represented by a full **A** and **R**:

air-conditioned   airmail   aerial

ANTI-/ANTE-

A disjoined **AN** is written in the **T** position: ....

ante-room   antiquated   anticlimax   anticipate

Exercise 6.5

See how many times you can write each of the following ten-word sentences in one minute.

1 ....
2 ....
3 ....
4 ....
5 ....

ULTRA-

A disjoined full **U** is written on the line ..𝘜....:

ultra-modern   ultrasonic   ultra-violet   ultra-marine

UPPER-

A disjoined full **U** is written above the line ....:

uppermost   upper-cut

Upper may also be used in groupings:

upper storey   upper class   upper hand   upper region

Speed drives
Exercise 6.6

(30 words in 15 seconds = 120 wpm)

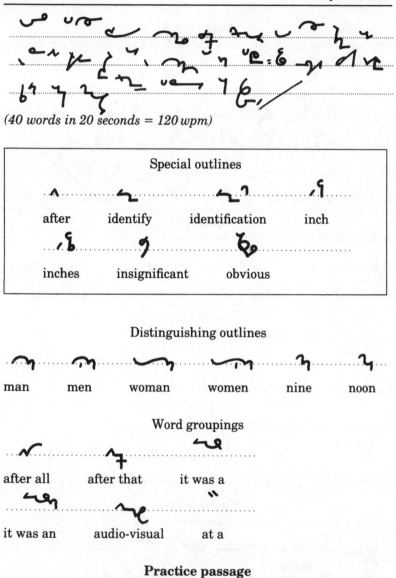

(40 words in 20 seconds = 120 wpm)

Special outlines

after	identify	identification	inch

inches	insignificant	obvious

Distinguishing outlines

man	men	woman	women	nine	noon

Word groupings

after all	after that	it was a

it was an	audio-visual	at a

Practice passage
Exercise 6.7
Read and prepare for dictation the following passage:

Company plans for the opening of a new shopping complex

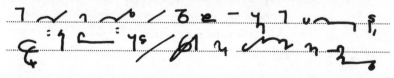

Speed hint

Always insert a vowel as it occurs between **R** and **M** in words such as:

ream   remainder   remedy

rim   romance   rumour

This will give more defined outlines.

Try writing the upward .... indicator before **P**, e.g.

appear .... appoint ..... aptitude ..., and so on, to give a good, sharp angle when written at speed.

Both these ideas will help you in transcription.

Dictation practice

Details concerning the sale of a house:

1 Letter from an estate agent to a client

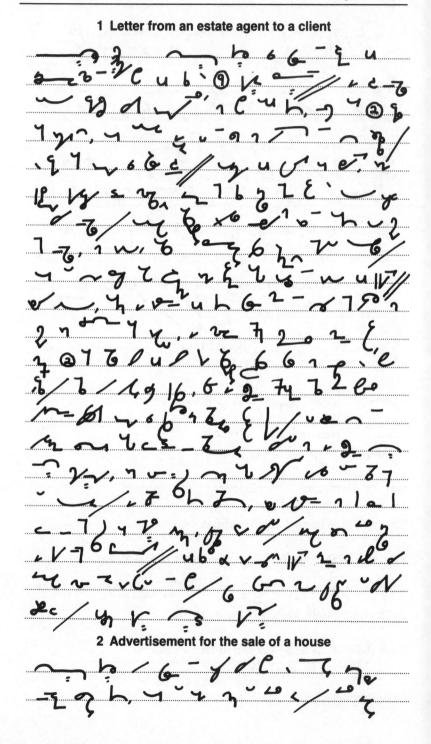

2 Advertisement for the sale of a house

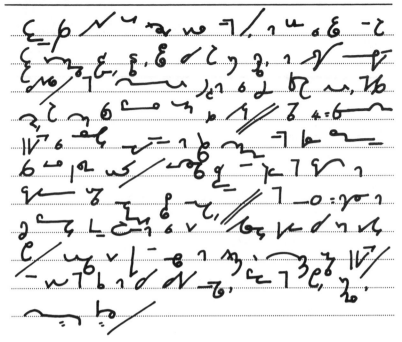

3 Letter from an estate agent to a client confirming an offer to buy

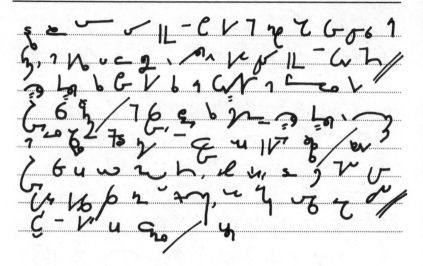

Top tip for this unit

If you have missed out words in your dictation, go over the passage
again to find out what you have omitted. Write and practise the
omitted portion several times before trying the dictated passage
again. The next time the passage is dictated, you should be able to
get it all down.

Unit 7
The business office

USEFUL BUSINESS GROUPINGS

Here are some more useful groupings for use in the office:

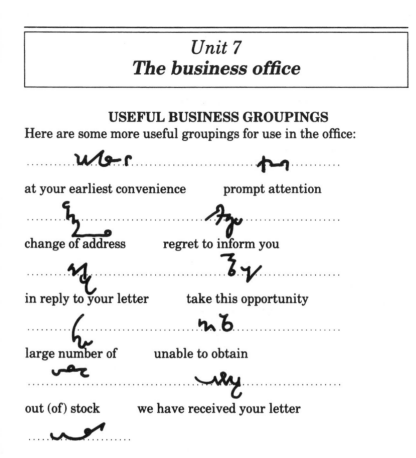

at your earliest convenience   prompt attention

change of address   regret to inform you

in reply to your letter   take this opportunity

large number of   unable to obtain

out (of) stock   we have received your letter

we were sorry

Speed drives
Exercise 7.1

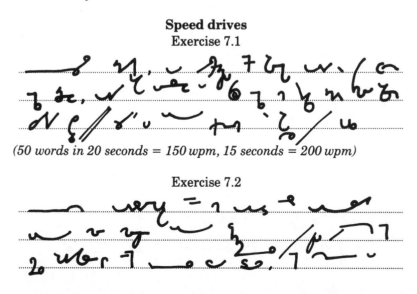

(50 words in 20 seconds = 150 wpm, 15 seconds = 200 wpm)

Exercise 7.2

(50 words in 20 seconds = 150 wpm, 15 seconds = 200 wpm)

Speed hint

Even when writing at speed, keep your outlines small and neat, not large and sprawling. You will write more quickly and it will be much easier to transcribe the dictation.

Dictation practice

The following dictation was taken by the Secretary to the General Manager of the local branch of Home and Away Motors, as part of the day's correspondence:

1 A circular letter – recipients' names will be inserted later

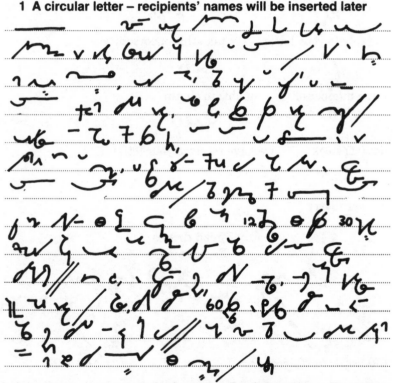

2 A reply to a customer who is requesting information. The letter contains three numbered points

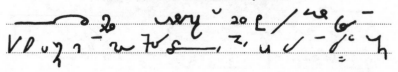

3 Memorandum to forecourt staff

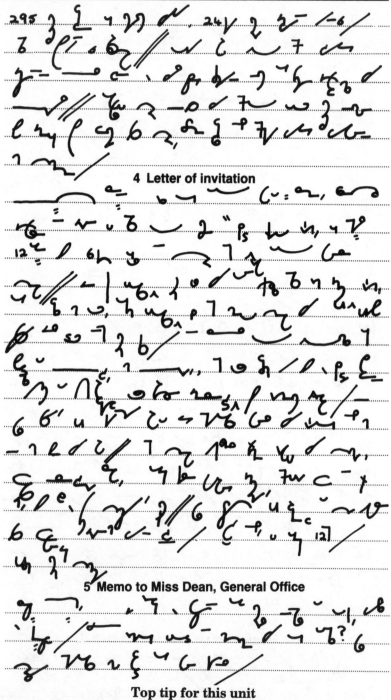

4 Letter of invitation

5 Memo to Miss Dean, General Office

Top tip for this unit

Always add a full stop when necessary, no matter how far behind you are. If you don't, your transcription will be muddled.

Unit 8
Another look at vowel endings

Remember that if a word ends with a sounded vowel, it is always inserted.

Exercise 8.1

Read and write the following words:

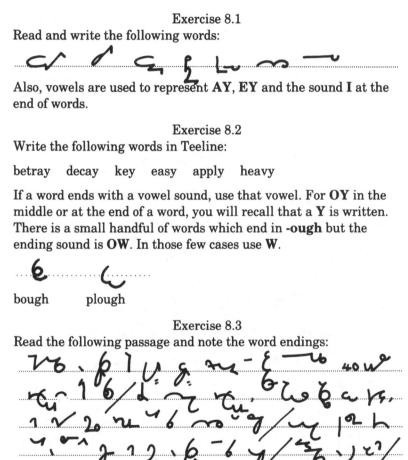

Also, vowels are used to represent **AY**, **EY** and the sound **I** at the end of words.

Exercise 8.2

Write the following words in Teeline:

betray   decay   key   easy   apply   heavy

If a word ends with a vowel sound, use that vowel. For **OY** in the middle or at the end of a word, you will recall that a **Y** is written. There is a small handful of words which end in **-ough** but the ending sound is **OW**. In those few cases use **W**.

bough   plough

Exercise 8.3

Read the following passage and note the word endings:

Exercise 8.4

Read the following passage containing disjoined vowel indicators for word endings, then take it down from dictation.

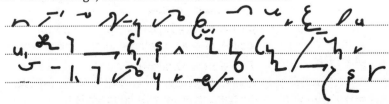

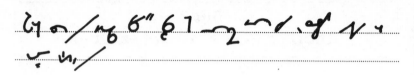

Exercise 8.5

Read this passage containing disjoined vowel indicators which
represent more word endings.

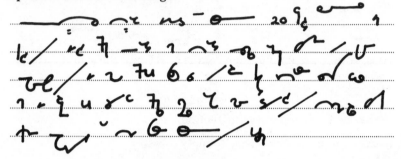

Exercise 8.6

Each of these sentences is 20 words long and contains words with
full vowel endings. See if you can write them all in one minute.
Say each word to yourself as you write it.

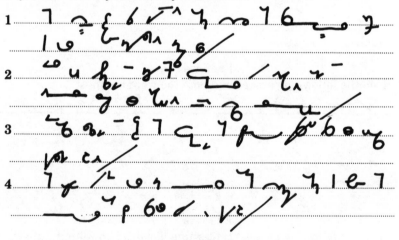

SUFFIXES:
-AFTER

In Unit 6 you used the full **A** for **AFTER-** as a prefix and in
groupings. A full disjoined **A** may also be used at the end of words
for **-AFTER**.

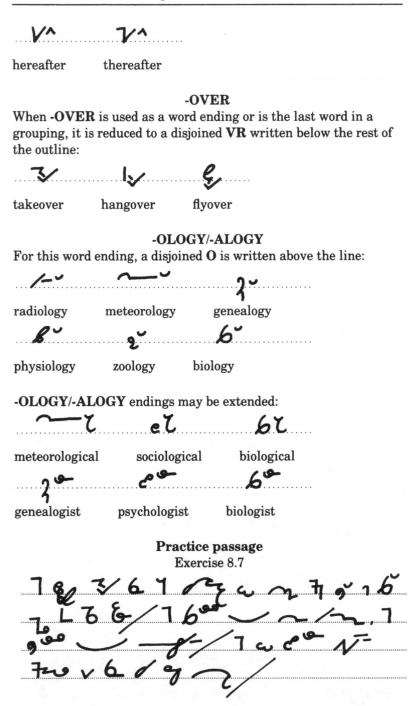

hereafter   thereafter

-OVER

When **-OVER** is used as a word ending or is the last word in a grouping, it is reduced to a disjoined **VR** written below the rest of the outline:

takeover   hangover   flyover

-OLOGY/-ALOGY

For this word ending, a disjoined **O** is written above the line:

radiology   meteorology   genealogy

physiology   zoology   biology

-OLOGY/-ALOGY endings may be extended:

meteorological   sociological   biological

genealogist   psychologist   biologist

Practice passage
Exercise 8.7

Special outlines

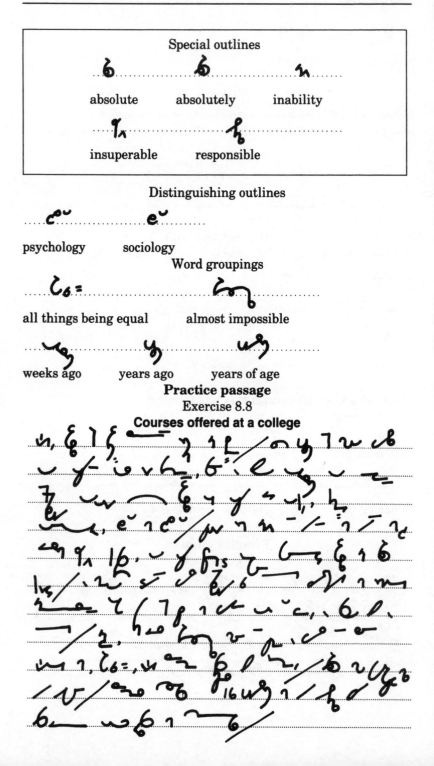

absolute   absolutely   inability

insuperable   responsible

Distinguishing outlines

psychology   sociology

Word groupings

all things being equal   almost impossible

weeks ago   years ago   years of age

Practice passage
Exercise 8.8
Courses offered at a college

Speed hint

Practise special outlines again and again until they become
automatic. This means you will then be able to write them
instantly, without thinking, when they are dictated as part of a
passage, again helping to increase your shorthand speed.

Dictation practice

Dictation from the proprietor of a health spa:

1 Letter to a prospective customer

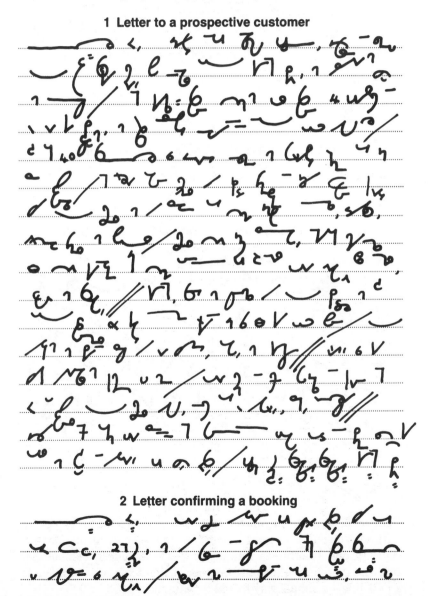

2 Letter confirming a booking

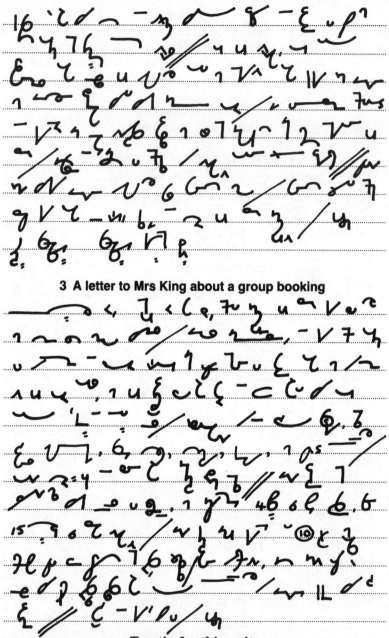

3 A letter to Mrs King about a group booking

Top tip for this unit

Remember to write disjoined letters and vowels close to the parent outline. You will then read them as part of the outline and not as a separate one. It also means that you will take up less room on the line and therefore reduce the number of times you need to move to a new line – a simple way to add to your speed!

Unit 9
Word contraction

Higher speeds can be achieved by contracting outlines, but care should be taken that these are fool-proof. If they are not fool-proof, errors and difficulties with transcription will occur. The old maxim 'If in doubt, write it out' still holds good here.

INT/IND

We have already omitted the **N** in words beginning with **INS** and

INC and in the special outline for **individual** .◠. Words

beginning with **INT** and **IND** can be dealt with in the same way:

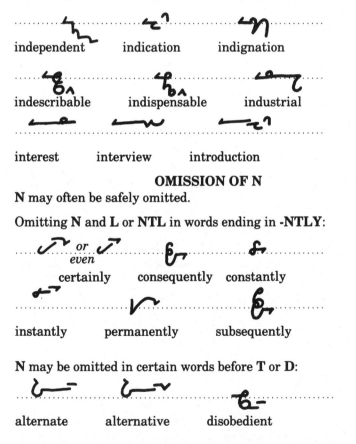

independent indication indignation

indescribable indispensable industrial

interest interview introduction

OMISSION OF N

N may often be safely omitted.

Omitting **N** and **L** or **NTL** in words ending in **-NTLY**:

or
even
certainly consequently constantly

instantly permanently subsequently

N may be omitted in certain words before **T** or **D**:

alternate alternative disobedient

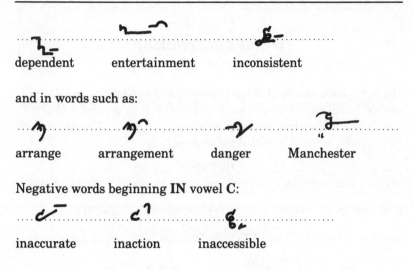

dependent   entertainment   inconsistent

and in words such as:

arrange   arrangement   danger   Manchester

Negative words beginning **IN** vowel **C**:

inaccurate   inaction   inaccessible

Words beginning **UN-**:

The **U** indicator is disjoined and written immediately in front of the first letter in the word. We have already met this disjoining in

the word **uneconomic**

unkind   unavoidable   unoccupied

unless   unalterable   unusual

-LY

Many words can be contracted by omitting the **L** in words ending **-LY**:

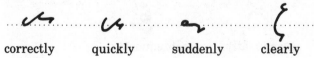

correctly   quickly   suddenly   clearly

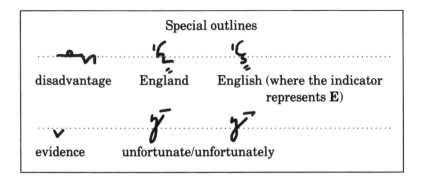

Special outlines

disadvantage   England   English (where the indicator
                                   represents **E**)

evidence   unfortunate/unfortunately

Distinguishing outlines

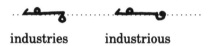

industries   industrious

Speed drives

See how many times you can write each sentence in half-a-minute
or a minute:

Exercise 9.1

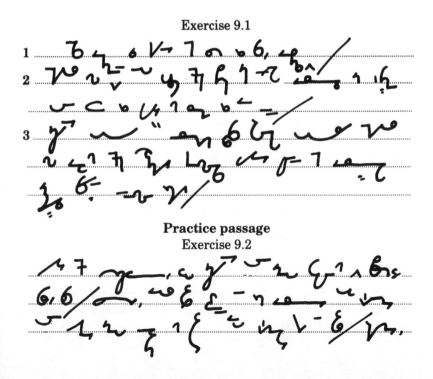

Practice passage
Exercise 9.2

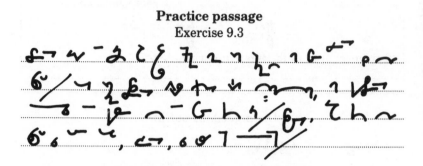

(50 words in 30 seconds = 100 wpm)

Practice passage
Exercise 9.3

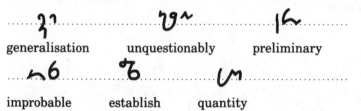

CONTRACTING LONG WORDS

Many long words can be contracted by leaving out the middle or the end of the word. Generally speaking, the longer the word, the safer it is to contract.

generalisation   unquestionably   preliminary

improbable   establish   quantity

Do remember that the beauty of Teeline is that it is quite correct to write any outline in full if you wish, but equally correct to contract words, *provided that* you can read them back correctly. But it is usually better to write proper names in full.

Exercise 9.4

Try writing contracted outlines for the following words:

notwithstanding   competitive   deliberate   corporation
consistently   extraordinary   irregular   signature
sympathetic   uncommunicative

Look in the Key (p. 128) for our suggestions, but you may have others that are equally good. The test is whether or not you can read the outlines back.

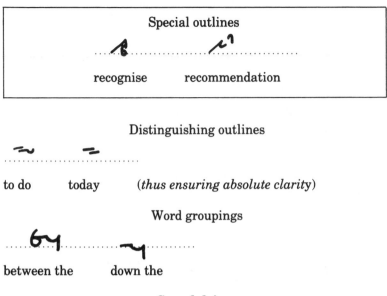

Distinguishing outlines

to do   today   (*thus ensuring absolute clarity*)

Word groupings

between the   down the

Speed drives
See how many times you can write these sentences in half-a-minute or a minute:

Exercise 9.5

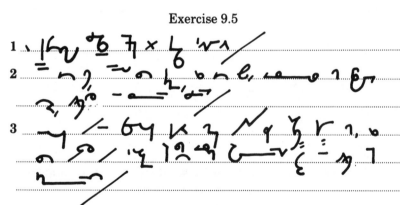

Speed hint
Paragraphs can be indicated in your notes by simply dropping down to the next line and carrying on writing from the same point as before. This method makes it easy to spot an outline in a particular paragraph.

Dictation practice
Correspondence from Personnel:

1 Memo from Personnel Officer to Social Club Secretary

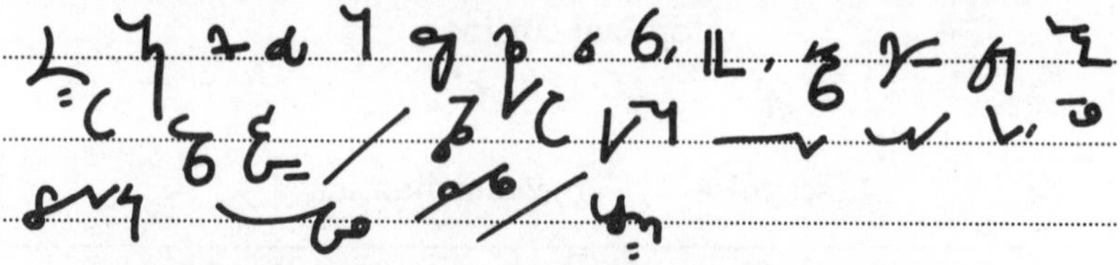

[shorthand]

2 Circular letter accompanying the memo above

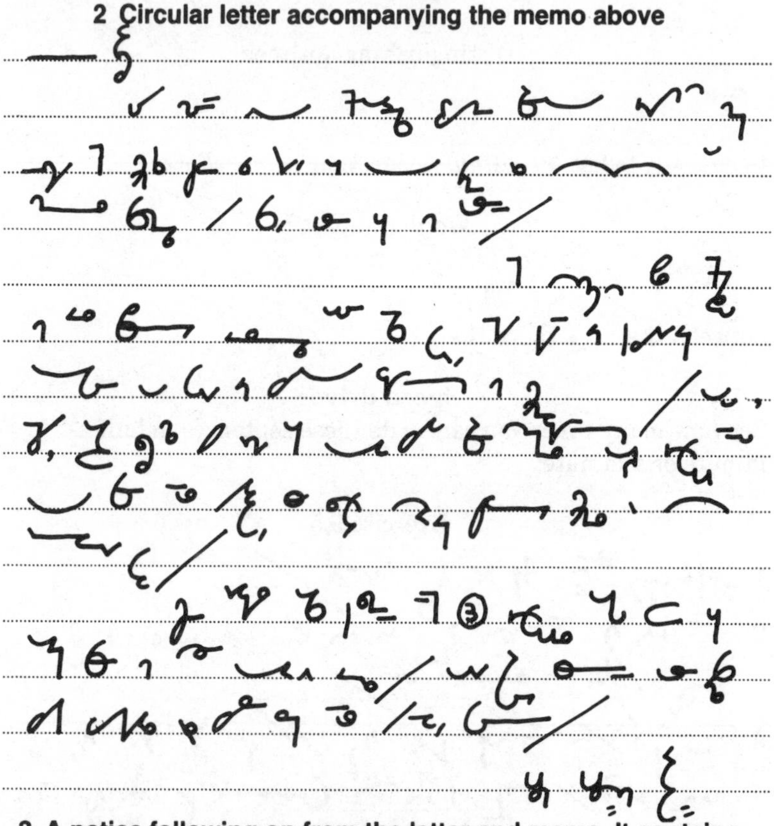

[shorthand]

3 A notice following on from the letter and memo. It contains three numbered points

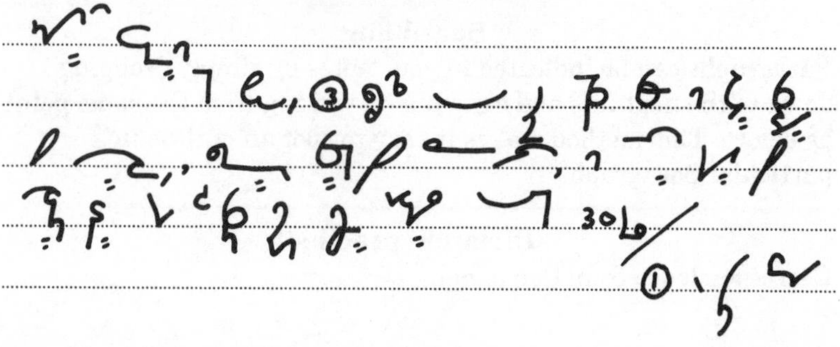

[shorthand]

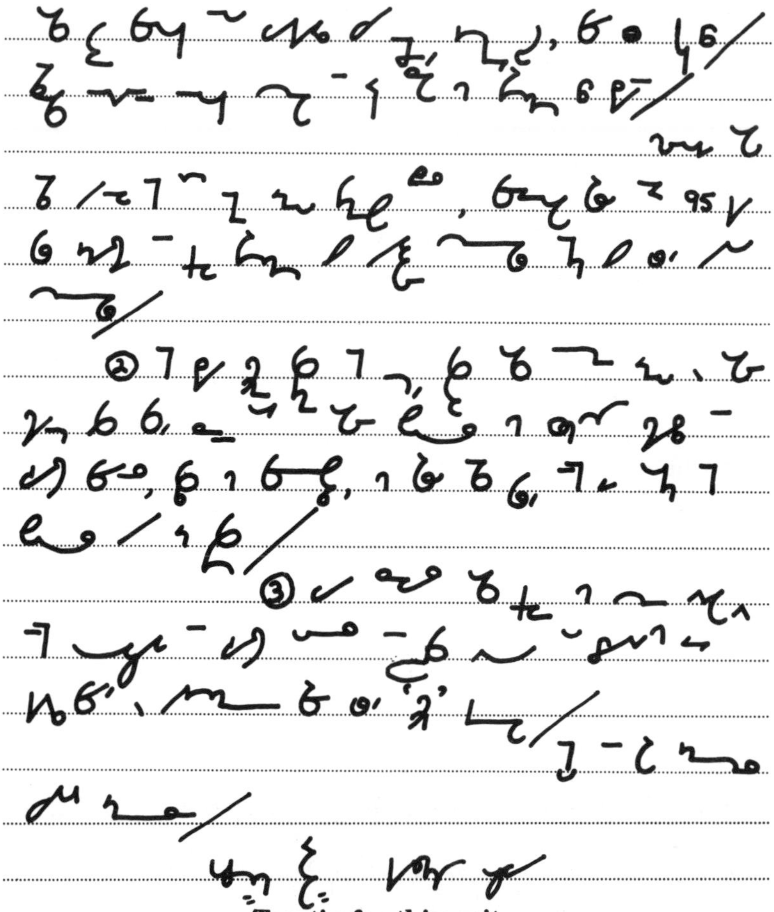

(shorthand outlines)

Top tip for this unit

Avoid using contractions or 'short cuts' that may not be completely safe when reading back. You can be sure they will lead to disaster! If you follow the hints given in this unit, you are on the right lines.

You can use many useful blends in Teeline to speed up your writing.

Exercise 10.1
Test yourself by writing the following words in Teeline, concentrating on the various blends.

F blends
   fulfil   frequency   reflect   refinement

X blends
   exemption   expressed   exerted   fixture

V blends
   evade   vendor   involve   virtue

P blends
   pavilion   publicity   complication   pleasant

RFR – when **R** is followed by **F** then **R** again, the blend is *not* used:

refrain   refresh   refurbish   refrigerate   referral

FW/WF – **F** is blended with **W** and written inside the curve

, but the version may be used if preferred:

  few   wife   wafer

Speed drive
Exercise 10.2

(40 words in 20 seconds = 120 wpm)

WORD ENDINGS:
-FULNESS: 6 .....

When **-FULNESS** ends a word it is reduced to **FLS** and written disjoined after the first part of the outline:

forgetfulness	carefulness	thankfulness

hopefulness	restfulness	usefulness

Note: When **fullness** is used as a complete word it is written in full

as 6 ....

Exercise 10.3

Read the following sentences:

1

2

WORD ENDINGS:
-LESSNESS/-LOUSNESS: .... 6 ...

Similarly, **-LESSNESS** or **-LOUSNESS** at the end of a word is reduced to a disjoined **LS**:

cheerlessness	helplessness	carelessness

fearlessness	thoughtlessness	callousness

Exercise 10.4

Read the following sentences:

1

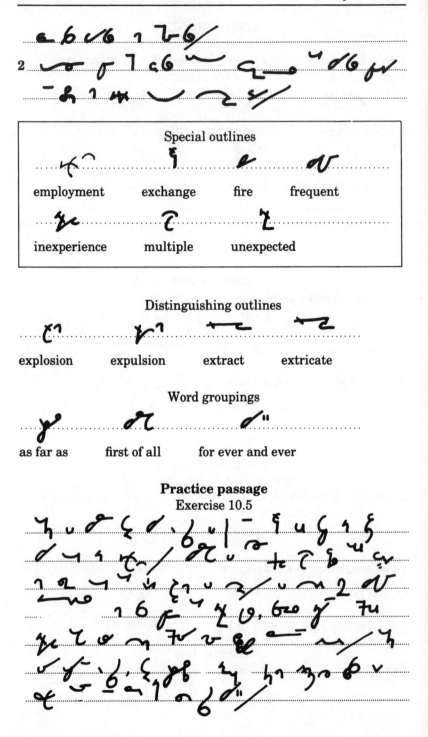

Special outlines

employment	exchange	fire	frequent

inexperience	multiple	unexpected

Distinguishing outlines

explosion	expulsion	extract	extricate

Word groupings

as far as	first of all	for ever and ever

Practice passage
Exercise 10.5

Speed hint

When a word starts with a small letter (such as **c** or **s**), a horizontal stroke or a vowel and is followed by **P**, write the **P** through the line. The word is then much more easily transcribed and not confused with words containing **H**. Examples include:

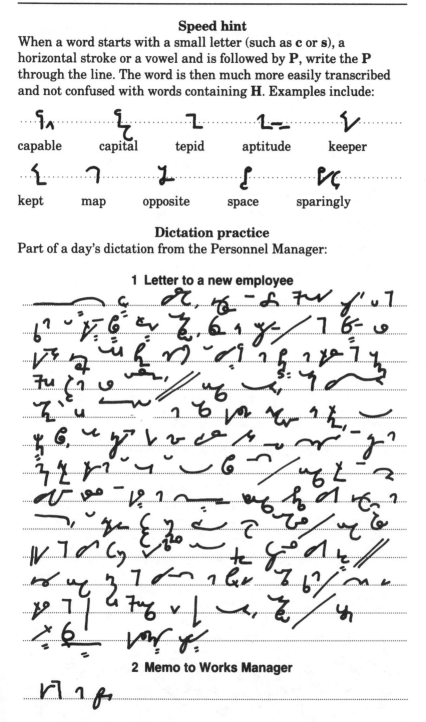

| capable | capital | tepid | aptitude | keeper |

| kept | map | opposite | space | sparingly |

Dictation practice

Part of a day's dictation from the Personnel Manager:

1 Letter to a new employee

2 Memo to Works Manager

3 Notice from Personnel Manager to all staff

(shorthand outlines)

4 Memo to all office staff

(shorthand outlines)

Top tip for this unit

If you cannot read a particular word when transcribing your
shorthand, read the rest of the sentence for meaning first and you
may find the word will come to mind. Very often, only one word is
appropriate to the sense of the passage where you have left a gap.

Unit 11
More about M, L and W

L AND LR
To recap, full **L** is normally used, but it is shortened and written downwards before **C**, **G**, **M** and **N** and upwards after **G**, **H** and **P** to give neater outlines. This also applies to the **LR** blend.

Exercise 11.1
Speed drive on letter L – notice which form of L is used

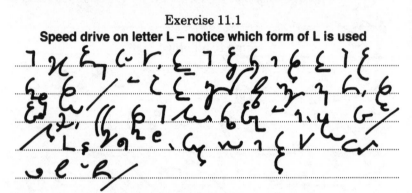

(60 words. Aim at writing in 30 seconds which is 120 wpm)

WORD ENDINGS:
-ALITY/-ELITY/-ILITY/-OLITY
Unless this ending follows **B**, it can be represented by a disjoined upward **L** written in or towards the **T** position.

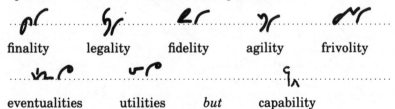

finality	legality	fidelity	agility	frivolity

eventualities	utilities	*but*	capability

-ARITY/-ERITY/-ORITY
This ending uses a disjoined **R** again written in or towards the **T** position.

hilarity	sincerity	minority

seniority	authority	priorities

M, -MENT AND MR

Check the way you are writing **M**. Is it shallow? ... ◠ ...

To recap, a small disjoined **M** written in the **T** position and close to the rest of the word gives the ending -**MENT**. **R** and **L** may be added for -**MENTARY** and -**MENTAL**. However, the word **meant**

standing alone should be written in full: ... ∿ ...

M can also be lengthened to add **R** and this becomes the **MR** blend: ⌒ .

Exercise 11.2
Speed drive on letter M

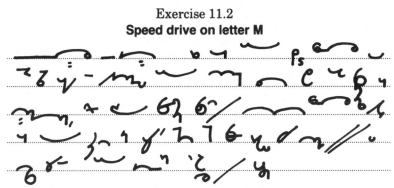

(60 words. Aim at writing in 30 seconds which is 120 wpm)

PREFIXES:
MAGNA-/MAGNE-/MAGNI-

These prefixes are represented by **MG** .⌒. disjoined, and written on the line:

magnanimous   magnetic   magnificent   magnify

..... ⌒. .....

magnolia

MB/BM

B may also be reduced to a circle before or after **M**:

MB = . ⌀ ...

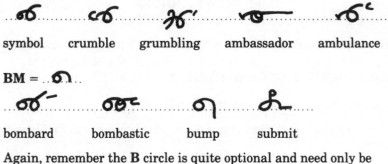

symbol   crumble   grumbling   ambassador   ambulance

BM =

bombard   bombastic   bump   submit

Again, remember the **B** circle is quite optional and need only be used if you wish.

W AND WR

Check the way you are writing **W**. Is it shallow and the upside-

down image of **M**? ﹀ To add **R**, lengthen it: ﹀

When joining **R** or **D** to **WK** or **WRK**, it is far easier to substitute **C** for **K**:

weaker   wicked   worker   worked

Exercise 11.3
Speed drive on letter W

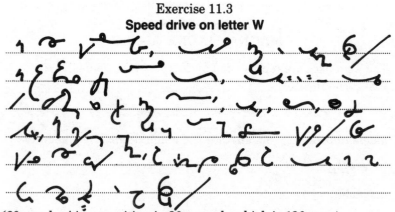

(60 words. Aim at writing in 30 seconds which is 120 wpm)

WORD ENDING:
-WIDE

The small **W** used as a word ending can also represent **-WIDE**, in addition to **-WARD/-WORD/-WOOD**:

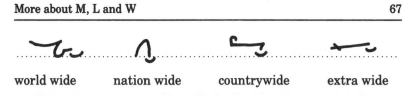

world wide   nation wide   countrywide   extra wide

The small **W** is *only* used as a suffix.

The word **wide** standing alone is written in full: ⌣ ....

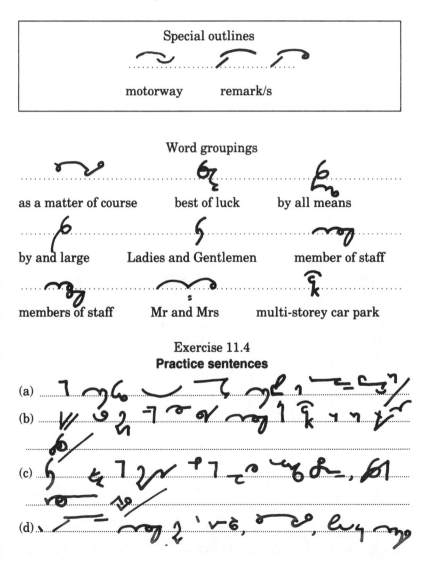

Special outlines

motorway   remark/s

Word groupings

as a matter of course   best of luck   by all means

by and large   Ladies and Gentlemen   member of staff

members of staff   Mr and Mrs   multi-storey car park

Exercise 11.4
Practice sentences

(a)

(b)

(c)

(d)

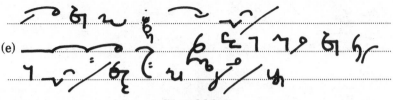

(e)

Speed hint

If you find you are unable to read an outline, when you eventually
discover what the word is (see Exercise 1.2), write the outline
several times together with the words on either side of it. Each
time write the words a little faster before taking the passage down
again.

Dictation practice

Mr and Mrs Taylor decide to go on a cruise:

Names of countries and towns mentioned in the dictation passages
are given here and you may like to practise these first.

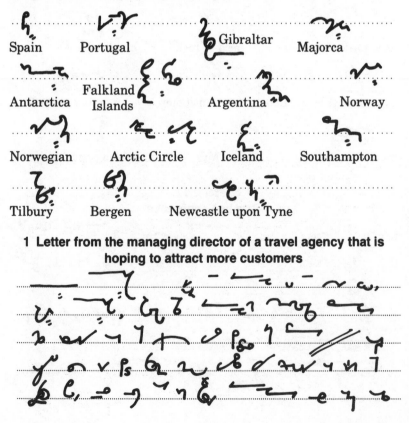

Spain   Portugal   Gibraltar   Majorca

Antarctica   Falkland   Argentina   Norway
               Islands

Norwegian   Arctic Circle   Iceland   Southampton

Tilbury   Bergen   Newcastle upon Tyne

1 Letter from the managing director of a travel agency that is hoping to attract more customers

2 Letter from Mr Stephen Naylor to the Sales and Marketing Manager of Aqua Travel, Short Street, Cambridge

3 Reply to Mr and Mrs Naylor from Aqua Travel

4 Confirmation of booking

5 Cancellation of booking

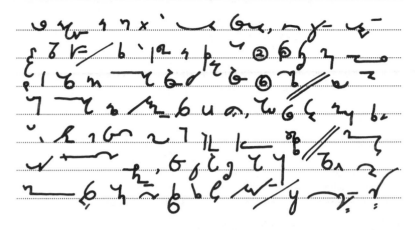

Top tip for this unit

Check size and shape of:

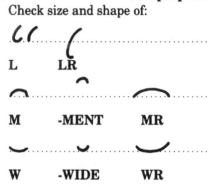

L   LR

M   -MENT   MR

W   -WIDE   WR

Remember to write **S** inside curves and outside circles.
Occasionally the shape is slightly elongated to make an easier
joining.

Exercise 12.1

Test yourself by writing the following words in Teeline:

suggested	surrender	supplement	
discrepancy	salesman	disclose	
illustrations	substitute	best	substance

Remember that **S** may be used for **Z** in the middle of a word:

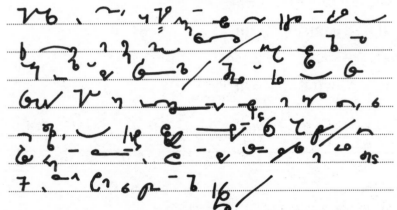

ozone	azure	lazy	brazen

Practice passage
Exercise 12.2

PREFIXES: SEMI-

A disjoined **S** on the line is used to represent the prefix **SEMI-**:

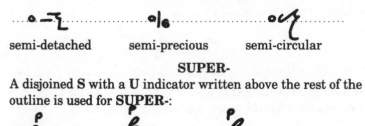

semi-detached	semi-precious	semi-circular

SUPER-

A disjoined **S** with a **U** indicator written above the rest of the
outline is used for **SUPER-**:

superfine	superfluous	superficial

Exercise 12.3

Read the following sentences:

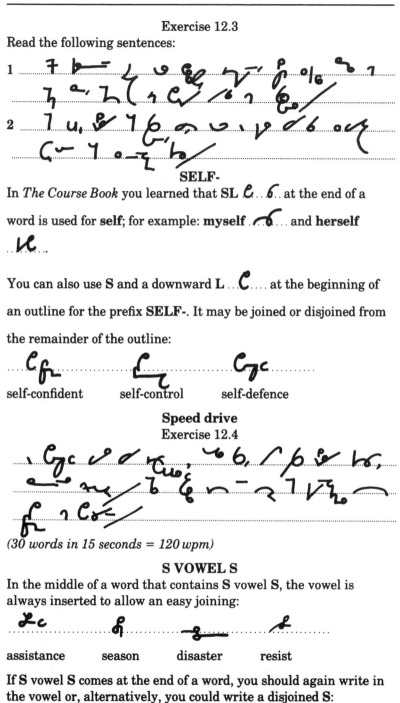

SELF-

In *The Course Book* you learned that **SL** ℓ $\mathscr{6}$ at the end of a

word is used for **self**; for example: **myself** $\mathscr{6}$ and **herself**

$\mathcal{K}$

You can also use **S** and a downward **L** $\mathcal{C}$ at the beginning of

an outline for the prefix **SELF-**. It may be joined or disjoined from

the remainder of the outline:

self-confident   self-control   self-defence

Speed drive
Exercise 12.4

(30 words in 15 seconds = 120 wpm)

S VOWEL S

In the middle of a word that contains S vowel S, the vowel is
always inserted to allow an easy joining:

assistance   season   disaster   resist

If S vowel S comes at the end of a word, you should again write in
the vowel or, alternatively, you could write a disjoined S:

.../6/... or ..6...   .../r/... or ..r/...   ...6'... or ..6o.
basis   emphasis   buses

.../6/... or .../6o..   .../6/... or ...1o.   .../16/... or ...16o.
consensus   possess   purchases

.../16/... or .../16o.   .../6/... or ...6o...
premises   successes

Remember that this is only a suggestion and can be discarded if
you prefer the first method. It is very useful in groupings however:

Special outlines			
6	6	8l	l6
access	because	successful	superb

Word groupings

.../7/... or ..7o...   .../9/... or ...7p.   .../7/... or ..7o.
this is   this is the   that this is

.........or .../7/..................
if this is the

Practice passage
Exercise 12.5

Speed hint

Make sure you are thoroughly familiar with all prefixes and suffixes as their use can make a long word into a short outline, and therefore increase your shorthand speed.

Dictation practice

Correspondence from the Managing Director of a software training company:

1 Memo to the Training Manager from the Managing Director about making a video

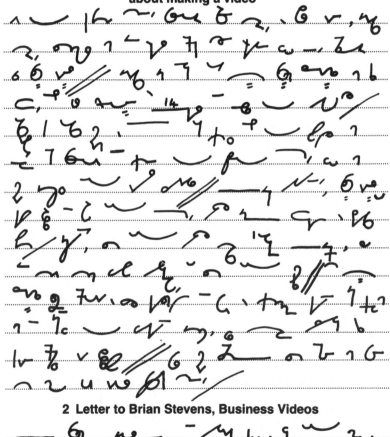

2 Letter to Brian Stevens, Business Videos

3 Memo from the Managing Director to the Training Manager

4 Letter from the Training Manager to a prospective client

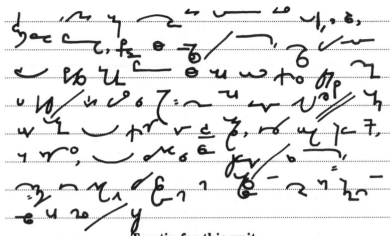

Top tip for this unit

When first taking down dictation, try short passages first, then
gradually build up your stamina by taking down progressively
longer passages. It is a good idea to split the passage to be dictated
into sections, practise them individually, and then practise the
whole passage. In this way you have more chance of being able to
write down the complete passage.

Unit 13
J and G

We already know that **J** and **G** are interchangeable, except at the beginning of a word. Use whichever form you find easiest.

WORD ENDINGS:
-JECT/-JECTION

Words ending in **-JECT** or **-JECTION** can be abbreviated, thus avoiding a difficult outline:

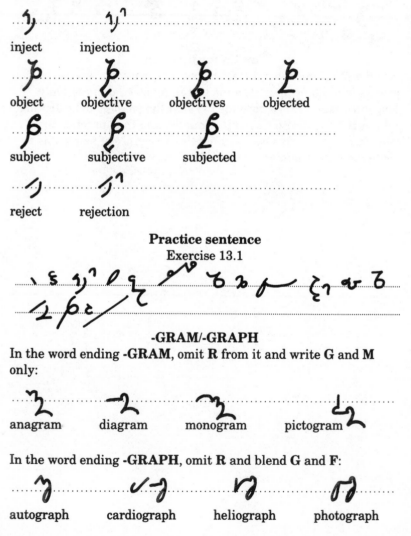

inject   injection

object   objective   objectives   objected

subject   subjective   subjected

reject   rejection

Practice sentence
Exercise 13.1

-GRAM/-GRAPH

In the word ending **-GRAM**, omit **R** from it and write **G** and **M** only:

anagram   diagram   monogram   pictogram

In the word ending **-GRAPH**, omit **R** and blend **G** and **F**:

autograph   cardiograph   heliograph   photograph

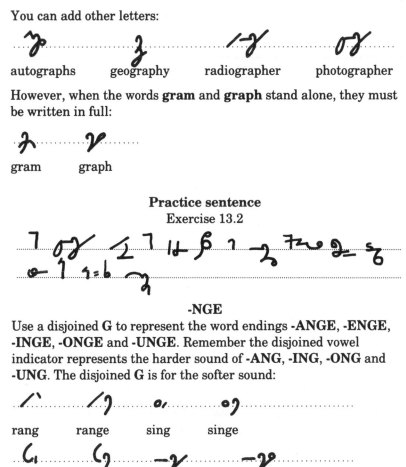

You can add other letters:

autographs   geography   radiographer   photographer

However, when the words **gram** and **graph** stand alone, they must be written in full:

gram   graph

Practice sentence
Exercise 13.2

-NGE

Use a disjoined **G** to represent the word endings **-ANGE**, **-ENGE**, **-INGE**, **-ONGE** and **-UNGE**. Remember the disjoined vowel indicator represents the harder sound of **-ANG**, **-ING**, **-ONG** and **-UNG**. The disjoined **G** is for the softer sound:

rang   range   sing   singe

lung   lunge   danger   dangerous

strange   stranger   strangely   strangeness

lounge   lounger   plunge   plunging

dungeon   Stonehenge

(*Note:* In Unit 9 **danger** is written as ⟍ᴨ ... This is all part of

Teeline's charm. Either outline is correct. *You* choose.)

Practice sentence
Exercise 13.3

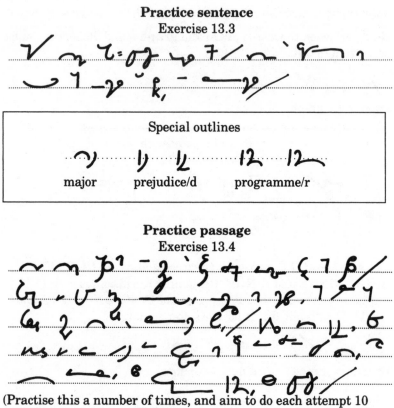

Special outlines

major   prejudice/d   programme/r

Practice passage
Exercise 13.4

(Practise this a number of times, and aim to do each attempt 10
seconds quicker than the last.)

Speed hint
Train yourself to think quickly. If your knowledge of Teeline
theory is sound, you will have 'immediate recall'.

Dictation practice
The Director of a Property Enquiry Agency dictates to his
secretary:

1 A memo to reception

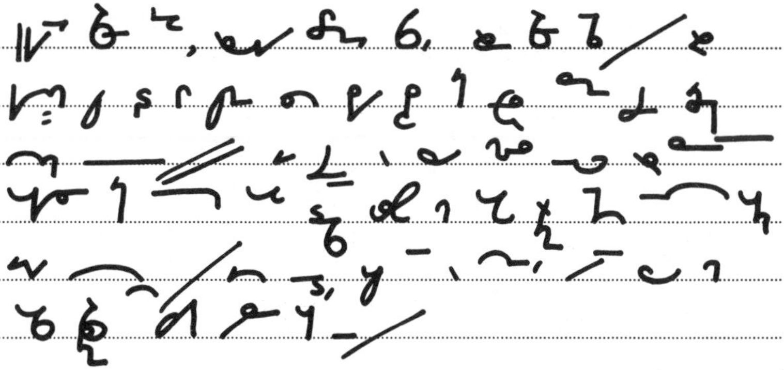

2 An article to be produced as a leaflet about living in Florida

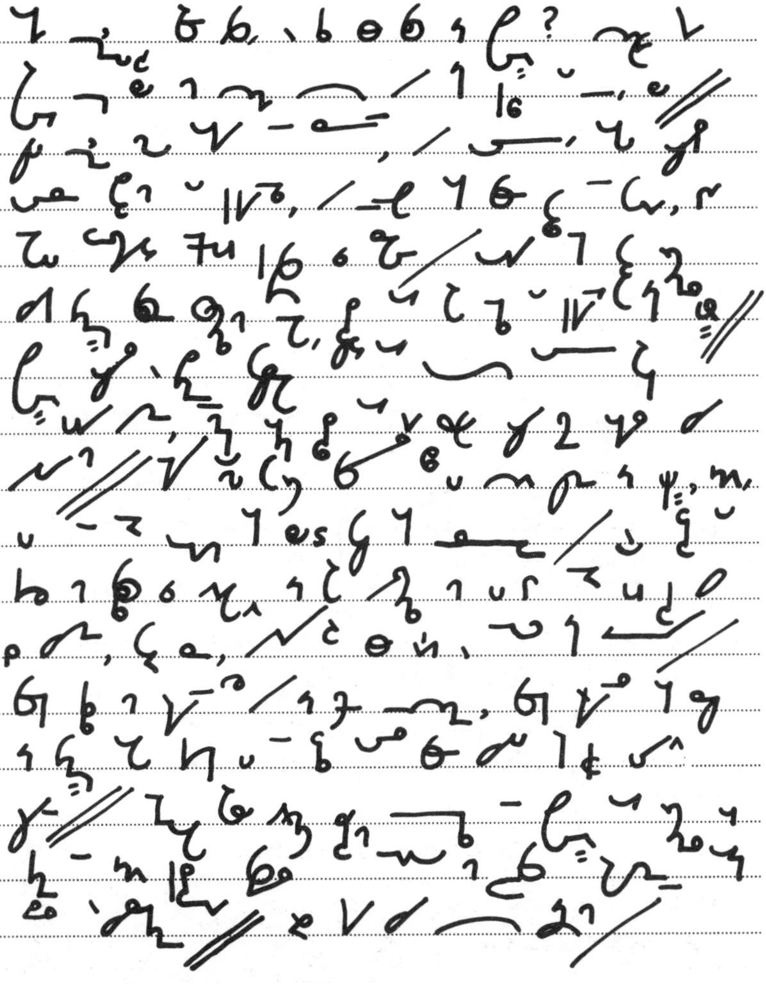

3 An article about time share to be produced as a leaflet entitled 'The Pros and Cons of Time Share'

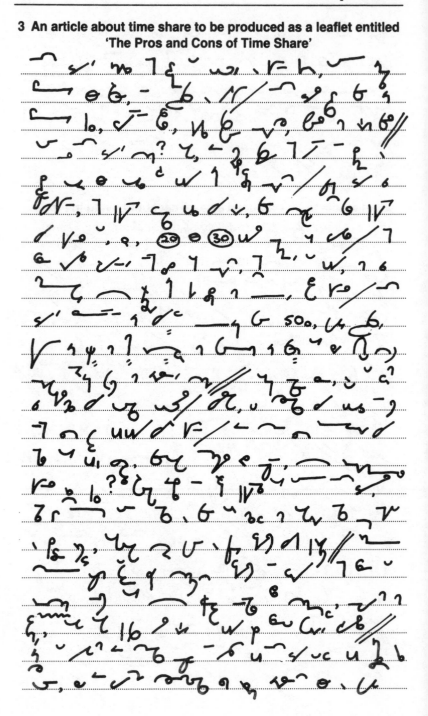

[Shorthand outlines]

4 An article to be produced as a leaflet entitled 'Listed Buildings'. Roman numerals should be used for the four numbered points

[Shorthand outlines with numbered points (i), (ii), (iii), (iv)]

Top tip for this unit

Remember the end product of shorthand is transcription. On completion you must check your transcription against the shorthand and also read through carefully to make sure it makes sense. Always keep your dictionary handy, and use it if in doubt.

You should be using Teeline's two **C** blends, **CM** and **CN**, wherever possible. These blends may be used either at the beginning, middle or end of an outline. **CNV** is a combination of **CN** with **V**.

Exercise 14.1
Test yourself by writing the following words in Teeline:

compact	accomplish	uncomplimentary	welcome
cancel	concerning	inconspicuous	economical
conversation	canvassed	convey	convert

Exercise 14.2
Read the following passage:

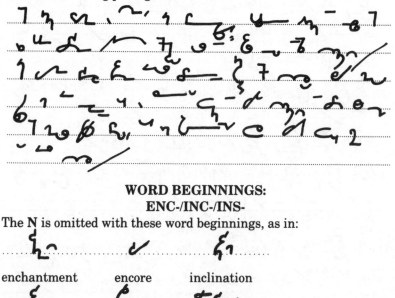

WORD BEGINNINGS:
ENC-/INC-/INS-
The **N** is omitted with these word beginnings, as in:

enchantment	encore	inclination
inclusive	insulate	instinctively

WORD ENDING:
-CH
There are some frequently written words ending in -**CH**. Because they are often used, the first part of the outline is written in the **T** position and the **CH** is omitted:

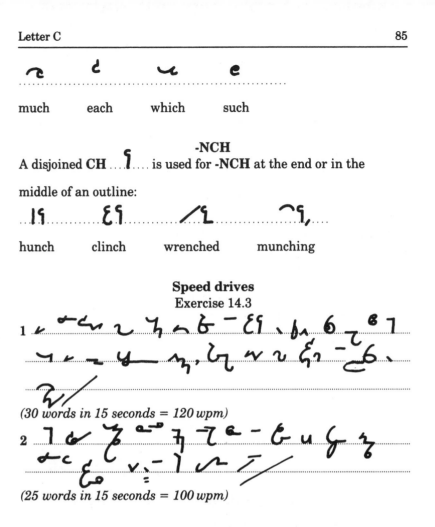

much   each   which   such

-NCH

A disjoined **CH** ....⌐.... is used for **-NCH** at the end or in the middle of an outline:

hunch   clinch   wrenched   munching

Speed drives
Exercise 14.3

1

(30 words in 15 seconds = 120 wpm)

2

(25 words in 15 seconds = 100 wpm)

MISCELLANEOUS TECHNICAL TERMS:
TECHNICAL

The word **technical** is represented by ...⌐... and **technological** is ...⊤... (note the shape).

technical college   technical training

technological age   technological skills

ELECTRONICS

The special outline for **electronic** ...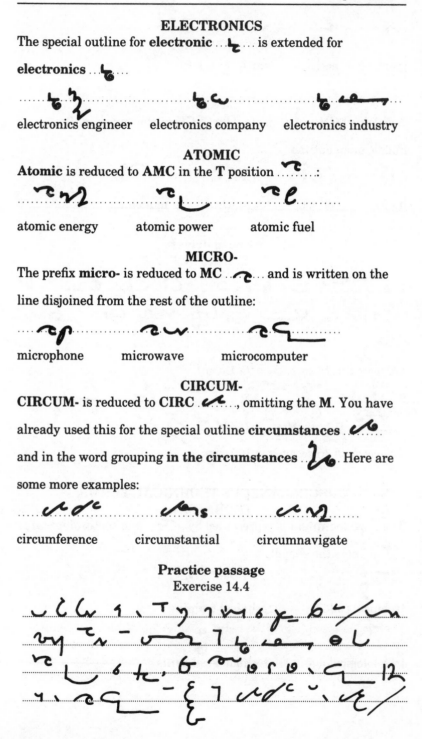... is extended for

electronics ......

electronics engineer   electronics company   electronics industry

ATOMIC

Atomic is reduced to **AMC** in the **T** position ....:

atomic energy   atomic power   atomic fuel

MICRO-

The prefix **micro-** is reduced to **MC** .... and is written on the

line disjoined from the rest of the outline:

microphone   microwave   microcomputer

CIRCUM-

CIRCUM- is reduced to **CIRC** ...., omitting the **M**. You have

already used this for the special outline **circumstances** ....

and in the word grouping **in the circumstances** .... Here are

some more examples:

circumference   circumstantial   circumnavigate

Practice passage
Exercise 14.4

Special outlines

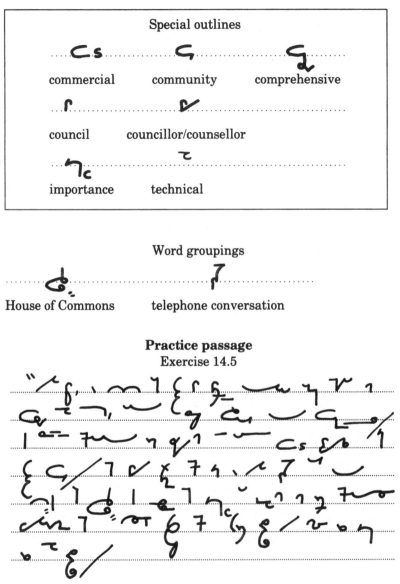

commercial   community   comprehensive

council   councillor/counsellor

importance   technical

Word groupings

House of Commons   telephone conversation

Practice passage
Exercise 14.5

SOFT C

Teeline represents both the hard **CK** sound and the soft **S** sound.
In pairs of short words it might occasionally be difficult to tell
which sound is intended. However, the context in which the word
appears should clarify this for you. Notice the soft **C** is used only in
the middle or at the end of an outline.

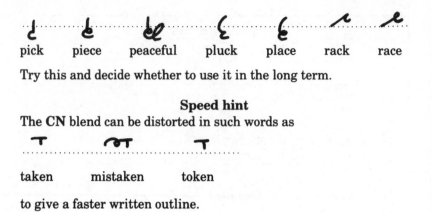

| pick | piece | peaceful | pluck | place | rack | race |

Try this and decide whether to use it in the long term.

Speed hint
The **CN** blend can be distorted in such words as

taken   mistaken   token

to give a faster written outline.

Dictation practice
Correspondence from the Sales Manager of Four Seasons Beauty, manufacturers of beauty products:

1 Letter to a new retail customer

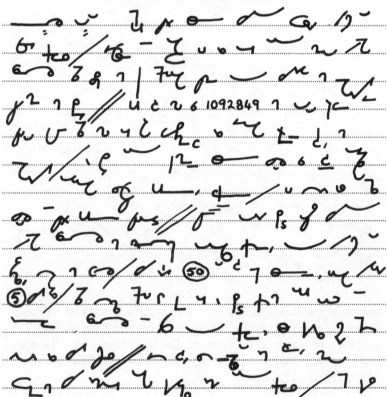

2 Letter to a customer confirming a competition win

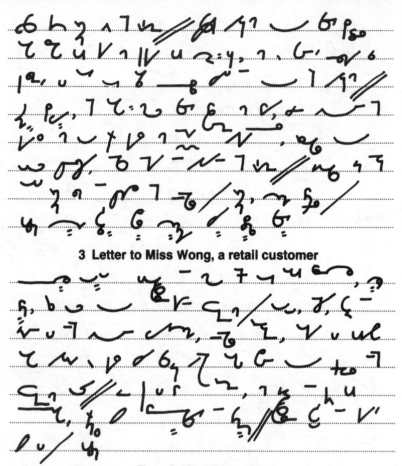

3 Letter to Miss Wong, a retail customer

Top tip for this unit

It is much better to have short periods of shorthand practice every
day rather than long ones once a week. Try to set aside some time
each day to write and learn outlines and to take dictation –
perhaps from an audio tape. It is a good idea to get into a regular
routine of practising at the same time each day. It then becomes a
habit and not a chore.

Unit 15
SH

The letter **S** represents the sound of **SH** in Teeline and is disjoined to represent the sound **-SHL** (or **-CIAL**, or **-TIAL**, however spelt). It is placed close to the end of the preceding stroke:

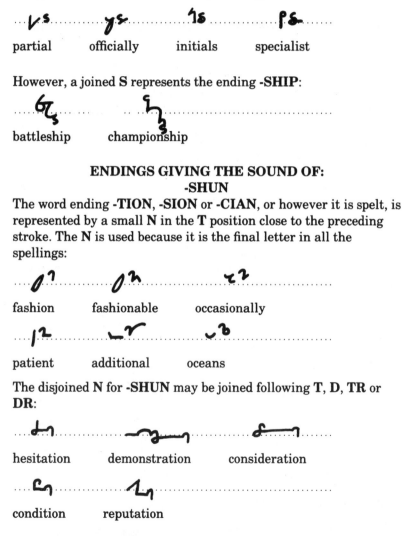

partial   officially   initials   specialist

However, a joined **S** represents the ending **-SHIP**:

battleship   championship

ENDINGS GIVING THE SOUND OF:
-SHUN

The word ending **-TION**, **-SION** or **-CIAN**, or however it is spelt, is represented by a small **N** in the **T** position close to the preceding stroke. The **N** is used because it is the final letter in all the spellings:

fashion   fashionable   occasionally

patient   additional   oceans

The disjoined **N** for **-SHUN** may be joined following **T**, **D**, **TR** or **DR**:

hesitation   demonstration   consideration

condition   reputation

This cuts down a hand movement.

-MENTATION

Words ending in -**MENTATION** have the -**SHUN** joined to the disjoined -**MENT**:

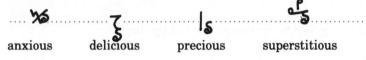

documentation   regimentation

-SHUS

Another way of using **S** is for the word ending that sounds like -**SHUS**, however it is spelt:

anxious   delicious   precious   superstitious

This makes for easier reading back than the normal ...**6**.... (e.g.

delicious ...**7**....).

Try it and then decide whether to use it in the long term.

Practice passage
Exercise 15.1

Read the passage and practise the words that you initially find difficult. Then see if you can write these 100 words in less than 1 minute at first take:

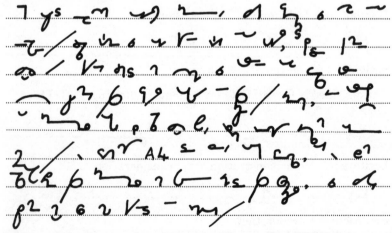

(100 words in 45 seconds = 150 wpm, 30 seconds = 200 wpm)

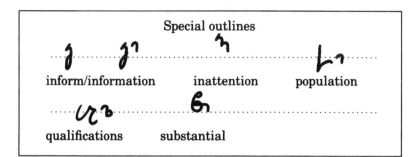

Special outlines

inform/information   inattention   population

qualifications   substantial

Distinguishing outlines

season   session   station   situation

Speed drives
Exercise 15.2

(a)
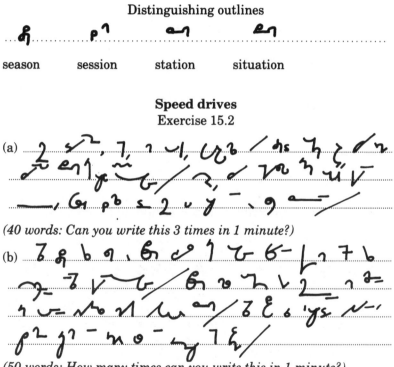

(40 words: Can you write this 3 times in 1 minute?)

(b)

(50 words: How many times can you write this in 1 minute?)

Speed hint
Aim always to get *something* down for *everything* dictated. Even if you only manage one or two letters in a word, it will help during transcription.

Dictation practice

Correspondence to and from a Garden Centre:

1 Circular letter

2 Letter from Barbara Sadler asking for information

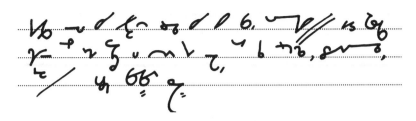

3 Letter of reply from Robert Eastwood, Managing Director

4 An article to accompany the previous letter

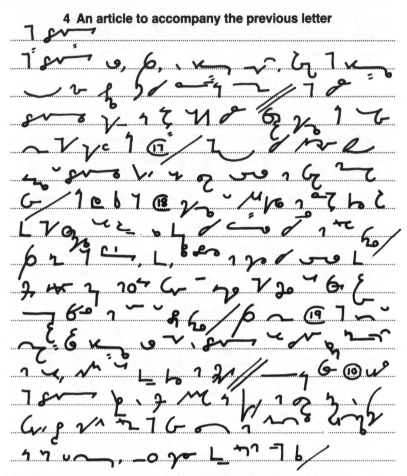

Top tip for this unit

Read Exercise 15.3 for extra speed hints. Either make a tape
yourself of this piece and play it through your personal stereo or
get a class mate, friend or relative to dictate it to you. For 100 wpm
each block of 10 words needs to be dictated in six seconds. In
addition to the speed hints given throughout this book, there are
several other things you can do to enable you to progress to higher
speeds.

Exercise 15.3

1 Plenty of dictation practice. Borrow a shorthand speed tape $/^{10}$ to
use at home, or get someone to dictate to $/^{20}$ you, or even try
making a tape yourself. You will $/^{30}$ need a stopwatch or a watch
with a second hand. $/^{40}$ At 60 wpm, 10 words are read in $/^{50}$ 10

seconds, at 120 wpm 10 words $/^{60}$ are read in 5 seconds and so on, and reading $/^{70}$ should be at an even speed for perhaps 3 or $/^{80}$ 4 minutes.

2 You must have the will to succeed $/^{90}$ and be able to stay motivated even though you appear $/^{100}$ to be 'stuck' at one certain speed. This hiccup is $/^{110}$ known as a speed plateau and almost all shorthand writers $/^{120}$ come to a plateau (dash) very often around the 70 $/^{130}$ wpm level and often again at around every $/^{140}$ 20 wpm above this speed. Don't worry (dash) $/^{150}$ it happens to everyone so don't become discouraged if you $/^{160}$ notice that each 10 word rise in speed seems to $/^{170}$ take longer to achieve than the previous 10 word rise. $/^{180}$ This is quite normal. The teacher or a textbook can $/^{190}$ give guidance, but ultimately it all comes down to you $/^{200}$ to persevere. By constant practice (dash) half an hour a $/^{210}$ day being more beneficial than 3 hours once a week $/^{220}$ (dash) and constant repetition, self-discipline is built up (dash) $/^{230}$ as it is with other skills such as learning to $/^{240}$ drive or learning to swim.

3 Writing speed depends not $/^{250}$ on the rapidity with which the hand moves across the $/^{260}$ page, but on the quickness of your thinking. Aim at $/^{270}$ developing a much wider vocabulary by reading anything and everything $/^{280}$ so that familiarity is developed with more unusual words that $/^{290}$ cause hesitation.

If despite all this the speed proves just $/^{300}$ too fast and your mind goes blank, don't panic with $/^{310}$ the effort of trying to remember, but start writing again $/^{320}$ the words the reader is actually speaking. It often helps $/^{330}$ to take a piece at a lower speed to get $/^{340}$ used to thinking more quickly of the more difficult words, $/^{350}$ or to take short high-speed bursts on easy material. $/^{360}$ Sometimes writing over the outlines of earlier attempts is a $/^{370}$ big help if you feel you have failed utterly at $/^{380}$ a higher speed.

Other things to try
Listen for the $/^{390}$ drop in voice and the slightly longer pause when the $/^{400}$ reader reaches the end of a sentence. Putting in full $/^{410}$ stops is essential.

Occasionally read through your notes, marking the $/^{420}$ errors. Ask yourself why you went wrong and which outline $/^{430}$ you missed. Practise the difficulties so the error is not $/^{440}$ repeated.

Don't slump over the desk with the non-writing $/^{450}$ hand propping up the head. An alert position leads to $/^{460}$ an alert mind.

Avoid making the margin wider and wider /[470] in an effort to keep up with the dictation. It /[480] means you are writing less and less on the page /[490] and thereby wasting time.

Check (colon) Are your strokes written /[500] with the sharpest possible angle?
Are you writing the outlines /[510] which come easiest to you and which carry your hand /[520] back to the writing line?
Are you positive they are /[530] keeping their shape and cannot be misread for something else? /[540]

Finally, the potential to reach high speed is dependent on /[550] good English, quick thinking, concentration, excellent memory, pen and outline /[560] control and a willingness to practise and be in constant /[570] training.

(571 words)

The Teeline Key to this dictation material is on pp. 147–8. It is a good idea to read the Teeline first prior to dictation.

Unit 16
Numbers, currencies, measurements and initials

NUMBERS

Numbers and currencies must be written quickly and be easily transcribed.

Always use figures for numbers under one hundred. Use Teeline outlines for larger numbers; it is quicker for round numbers, but for others use a combination of outlines and figures:

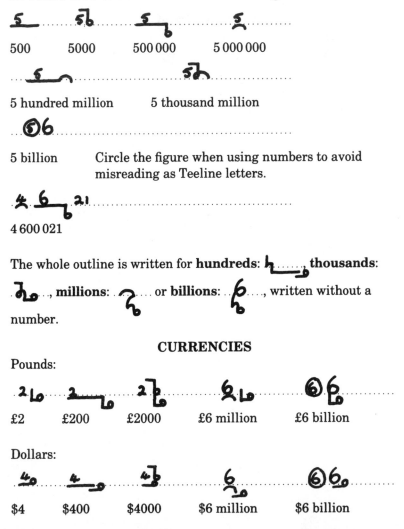

| 500 | 5000 | 500 000 | 5 000 000 |

5 hundred million   5 thousand million

5 billion   Circle the figure when using numbers to avoid misreading as Teeline letters.

4 600 021

The whole outline is written for **hundreds**: ⌐ **thousands**: ⌐, **millions**: ⌐ or **billions**: ⌐, written without a number.

CURRENCIES
Pounds:

| £2 | £200 | £2000 | £6 million | £6 billion |

Dollars:

| $4 | $400 | $4000 | $6 million | $6 billion |

Deutschmark:

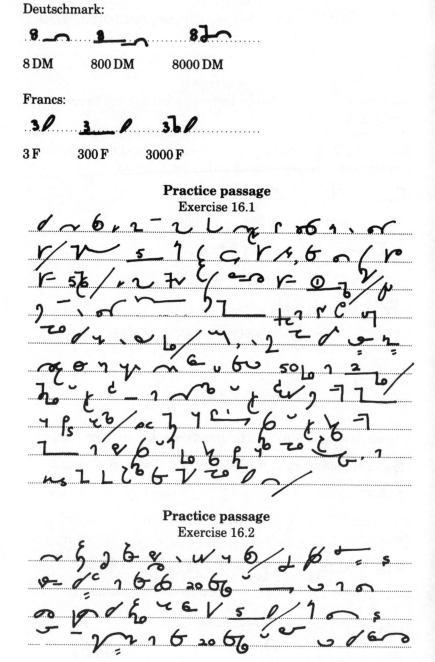

8 DM   800 DM   8000 DM

Francs:

3 F   300 F   3000 F

Practice passage
Exercise 16.1

Practice passage
Exercise 16.2

MORE CURRENCIES

Some more currencies are given below. If you take dictation with
yet different currencies, devise your own special outlines and
practise them.

	with number	*as in*		*without a following figure*
ECU		20 million ECUs	
peseta		5000 pesetas	
Belgian franc		800 Belgian francs	
Swiss franc		500 000 Swiss francs	
gilder		300 million gilders	
lira (plural lire)		3 billion lire	
escudo		50 escudos	
krone (plural kroner)		600 kroner	
drachma		10 000 drachmas	
yen (plural yen)		50 000 yen	
Irish punt		£28 000 Irish	

When currencies are written without a number, the full outline
should be written. However, if you frequently use some of these
currencies in your dictation, you may abbreviate them to suit your
own purposes.

MEASUREMENTS

Remember to omit the dividing line for fractions as in ½:

	with number	*as in*	
gram	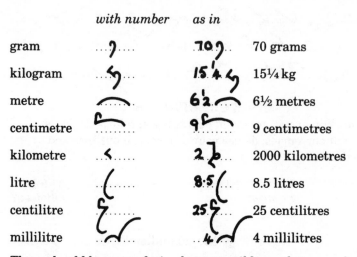		70 grams
kilogram			15¼ kg
metre			6½ metres
centimetre			9 centimetres
kilometre			2000 kilometres
litre			8.5 litres
centilitre			25 centilitres
millilitre			4 millilitres

There should be no confusion between gilder and gram or between krone and kilometre if the words are read in context.

Practice passage
Exercise 16.3

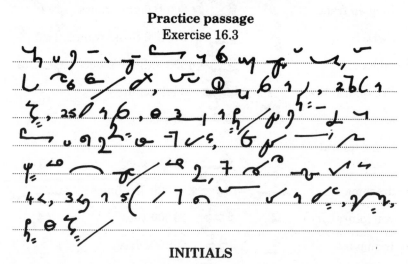

INITIALS

These days we use initials instead of the whole words for many things. In Teeline these initials are written either joined together or separately, but it is necessary to put .... underneath to show that they are capitals. Here are some of the most common ones you may be familiar with:

EC	...⌇...	European Community
NVQ	...⌇...	National Vocational Qualification
BTEC	...⌇...	Business and Technical Education Council
RSA	...⌇...	Royal Society of Arts
NHS	...⌇...	National Health Service
PAYE	...⌇...	Pay As You Earn
BASIC	...⌇...	Beginners All-Purpose Symbolic Instruction Code
DIY	...⌇...	Do It Yourself
AA	...⌇...	Automobile Association
PTA	...⌇...	Parent Teachers Association

PER CENT

Remember that **per cent** is represented by **PR** as in ..⌇.. (5 per cent) and **per cent per annum** is written with two Ps as in ..⌇.. (7 per cent per annum).

Word grouping

AGM ..⌇.. Annual General Meeting (..⌇.. indicates that the words are to be written in full).

Speed drives
Exercise 16.4

See how many times you can write each of these sentences in a minute.

1 ⌇

words (15)

2 ⌇

words (20)

3 ⌇

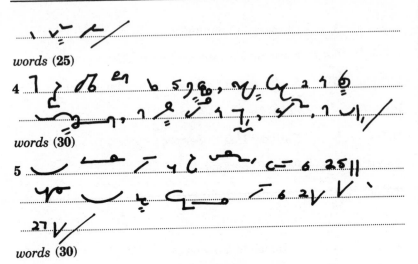

words (25)

words (30)

words (30)

Speed hint

Effective shorthand is very much dependent on the ability to think quickly. The sequence is: listening to the word, working out the outline, then writing it down. In fact, thinking of the outline takes longer than actually writing it. But when you practise your shorthand regularly, you reduce your thinking time – and your shorthand speed increases.

Dictation practice

Correspondence dictated by a bank manager:

1 Letter offering a mortgage to a customer

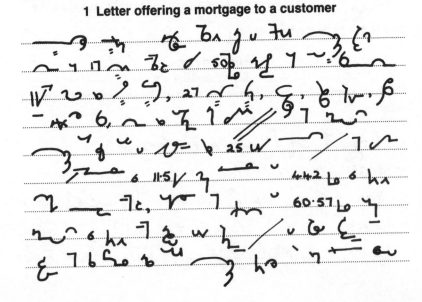

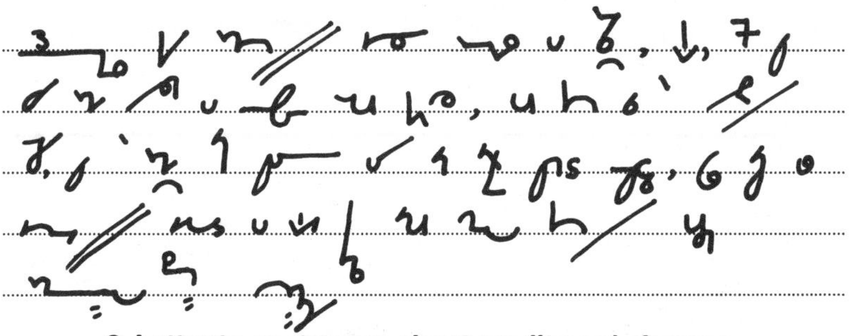

2 Letter to customers about credit card charges

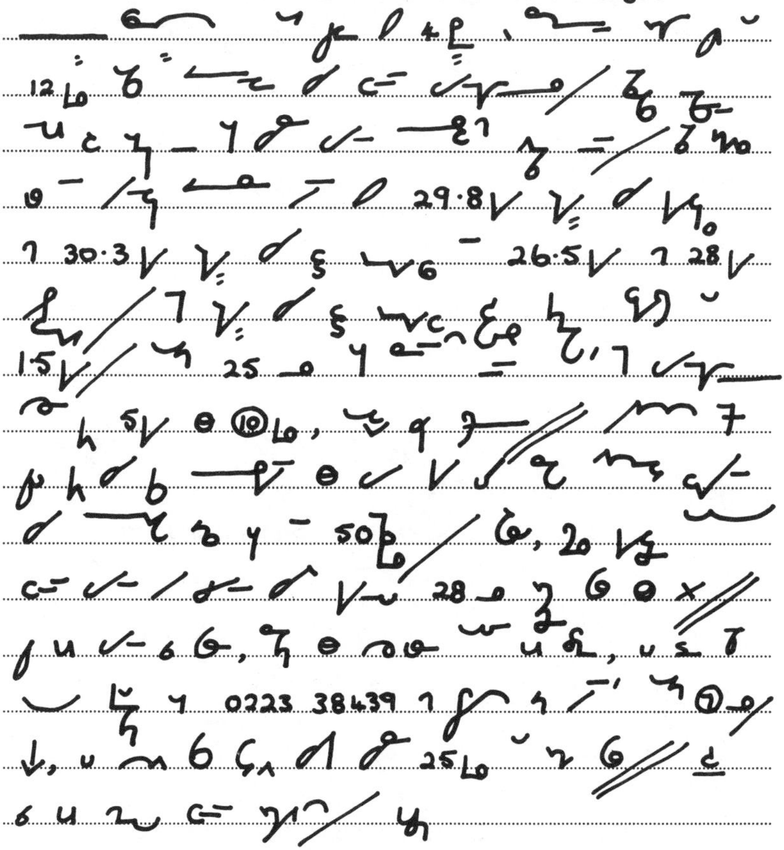

3 Letter to customers about savings schemes for children

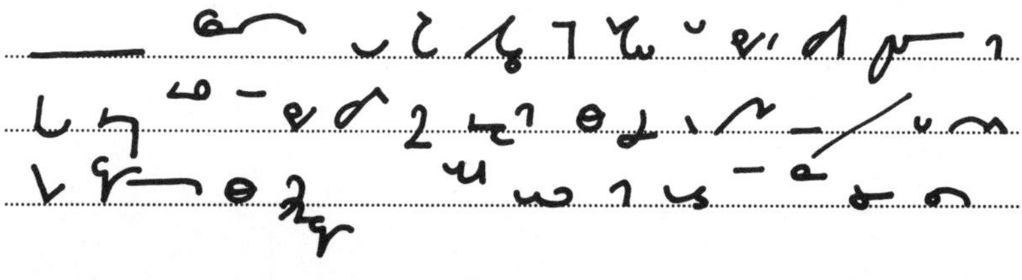

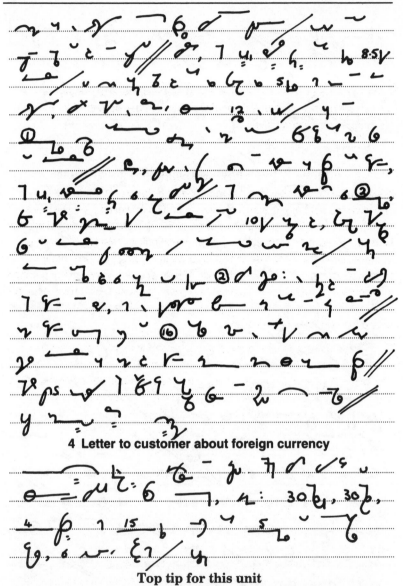

4 Letter to customer about foreign currency

Top tip for this unit

Always put the date on the page of your shorthand notebook. You will then be able to look back at your notes and identify the order in which correspondence or documents occur, or check when something was dictated.

Key

Note: Underlining in the Key indicates a special outline, a distinguishing outline, a word grouping or a point of theory which has appeared for the first time in the corresponding unit.

Exercise 1.1
Writing Teeline

Teeline may be written with a ballpoint, pencil or fountain /[10] pen, and choosing the right one to suit your own /[20] particular writing style will make writing and therefore transcription easier. /[30] Writing should be controlled; that is to say, there is /[40] no point at all in writing so quickly that the /[50] outlines become unreadable and lose their shape, so that you /[60] end up with no transcription at all or merely 'rubbish'. /[70] Make sure the Teeline letters are all in proportion, vowels /[80] are smaller than consonants, and the shape and size of /[90] the letters are maintained. By doing this you will be /[100] delighted to see speed following on quite naturally.

To improve /[110] speed try reading printed Teeline as quickly as possible, whenever /[120] you have a few spare moments (dash) reading each passage /[130] several times until there is no hesitation and each reading /[140] is quicker than the last. It is even more important /[150] to become familiar with your own notes, always reading everything /[160] you have taken down. It is best to aim at /[170] writing not less than twelve outlines to one line of /[180] your notebook. (**182**)

Exercise 1.2

When meeting a word you cannot read try the following. /[10] Change the Teeline letters into longhand. Does this skeleton suggest /[20] a word or words? Go back to the beginning of /[30] the sentence and read as far as the unknown word, /[40] omit the unknown word, and then carry on reading to /[50] the end of the sentence. What word would make sense /[60] in the gap? Does this word fit your skeleton outline? /[70] If not, what might be an alternative to the word /[80] you thought of? I am sure then that the unknown /[90] word will leap out at you to complete the sentence. /[100]

Do not spend much time pondering over the unknown word /[110] itself without reading on for context as described. (**118**)

Exercise 1.3

There will always be a need for a good shorthand /[10] writer, despite claims that machines are now a replacement. Some /²⁰ employers dislike dictating into a machine and prefer to have /³⁰ more time to think over what they wish to say. /⁴⁰ **(40)**

Exercise 1.4

Is it significant that my husband always starts to read /¹⁰ his Sunday newspaper with its many enclosures just as lunch /²⁰ is ready? **(22)**

Exercise 1.5

'Personnel', and 'Personal' are often confused. Personnel means a body /¹⁰ of employees, whereas personal means private or individual. **(18)**

Diamonds

One of Amsterdam's major attractions is a visit to a /¹⁰ diamond warehouse. It offers visitors an opportunity to see how /²⁰ a diamond is transformed from a rough, unattractive stone into /³⁰ a sparkling gem. Visitors may watch a film which lasts /⁴⁰ about 15 minutes showing the diamond being mined, cut, and /⁵⁰ finally shaped and polished. You can actually watch the finished /⁶⁰ product being mounted and set by experienced goldsmiths. A walk /⁷⁰ through the showrooms follows, where a superb display of diamonds /⁸⁰ and other jewellery worth a king's ransom can be seen /⁹⁰ and admired from a distance.

Expert advice is available at /¹⁰⁰ a reasonable charge should you wish your own personal jewellery /¹¹⁰ to be valued, and good trade-in rates are offered /¹²⁰ if you can afford to buy a more valuable stone. /¹³⁰ **(130)**

Exercise 2.1

Owing to the fact that our sales have been increasing /¹⁰ for a long time, three or four additional men or /²⁰ women are expected to be employed more or less immediately. /³⁰ **(30)**

Exercise 2.2

The fact of the matter is that for years and /¹⁰ years our sales representative travelled up and down the country /²⁰ visiting companies here and there, near and far and in /³⁰ out of the ordinary places to try to get orders. /⁴⁰ **(40)**

Exercise 2.3

Whether or not it is right or wrong the truth /¹⁰ is that when the rate of interest is increased, quite /²⁰ a lot of people cannot make ends meet, according to /³⁰ the newspapers, but somehow or other they seem to manage. /⁴⁰ **(40)**

Exercise 2.4

The <u>social committee</u> decided to <u>take on</u> more bar staff /[10] so that queueing would be reduced <u>as much as possible</u> /[20] in peak periods and members could purchase their <u>requirements</u> quickly. /[30] **(30)**

Exercise 2.5

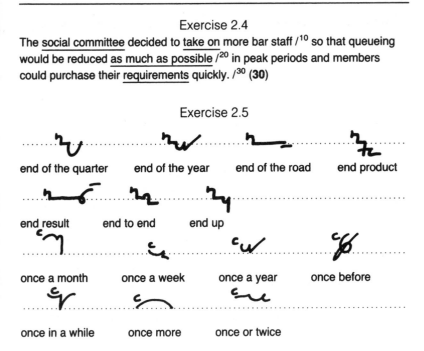

| end of the quarter | end of the year | end of the road | end product |

| end result | end to end | end up |

| once a month | once a week | once a year | once before |

| once in a while | once more | once or twice |

Exercise 2.6

<u>From the beginning</u> the <u>high street bank</u>'s legal service advises /[10] people wishing to set up a business on how to /[20] draw up their <u>Articles of Association</u> and <u>Memorandum of Association</u>. /[30] **(30)**

Exercise 2.7

<u>At the beginning</u> of the week the <u>royal visitor</u> arrived /[10] at the <u>railway station</u> in the <u>City of London</u> to /[20] open the <u>trade association</u> building near the <u>Bank of Pakistan</u>. /[30] **(30)**

Exercise 2.8

Memo to Secretarial Services Supervisor

At the <u>end of the week</u> I am going to /[10] the <u>City</u> for a few days on business and I /[20] would like the following tasks completed in my absence:

1 /[30]   <u>Articles of Association</u> to Smith Bros
2   Minutes of the /[40] <u>Finance Committee</u>
3   Draft letter to <u>the bank</u>
4   Travel /[50] arrangements from here to <u>New Street Station</u> for next Wednesday. /[60]
5   Book the usual room at the <u>Royal Hotel</u> for /[70] a meeting next Friday. **(74)**

1 Letter from Wedding Services Ltd, replying to an enquiry

Dear Mrs Harrison

Thank you for your enquiry about the /[10] services our company offers. As you will see from the /[20] attached brochure, we are a unique company offering a complete /[30] range of wedding services for that special day, taking all /[40] the worry from the shoulders of the bride, the groom /[50] and parents.

Our bridal boutique is full of many beautiful /[60] gowns for the bride and bridesmaids and we also offer /[70] a range of outfits for the bride's mother. Our customers /[80] are given a discount voucher from one of the country's /[90] leading jewellers to purchase their wedding rings.

On the Wedding /[100] Day we arrange the flowers, cars, cake and reception. We /[110] plan everything just as you require. It is always our /[120] aim to ensure the bride and groom have a really /[130] happy day.

If I may be of further assistance, please /[140] do not hesitate to contact me.

Yours sincerely

Mark Rogers /[150]

Wedding Services Ltd (**153**)

2 Letter to Mrs Harrison about the reception and flowers

Dear Mrs Harrison

Thank you for giving us the firm /[10] order for your daughter's wedding. When I spoke to you /[20] at the Annual Wedding Fayre held in the Town Hall /[30] last Saturday, you mentioned that the reception is to be /[40] for one hundred people, and as the bride and groom /[50] are vegetarians, the traditional wedding meal is not to be /[60] provided. I have spoken to the Catering Manager and I /[70] enclose a list she has drawn up of suitable dishes /[80] which you might like to consider.

The Edwardian theme the /[90] couple have chosen for the day will present no problems /[100] for the florist, who has studied flower arrangements from that /[110] period and can create the ideal bouquet for the bride, /[120] plus the attendants' posies and the flowers for the church /[130] and table decorations. Your daughter's wishes with regard to the /[140] cake have been noted and I have sent details to /[150] our cake specialist who will prepare designs for your approval. /[160]

I hope this answers your queries. We will do everything /[170] in our power to make your daughter's wedding a memorable /[180] occasion and I look forward to hearing from you.

Yours /[190] sincerely (**191**)

3 Memo to the Cake Decorating Supervisor from Mark Rogers

Mrs Harrison has just contacted me to order the cake /[10] for her daughter's wedding which is to be held on /[20] the first Saturday in December. The groom is a market /30 gardener and the couple are very much involved in show /40 jumping. Therefore, they would like a novelty cake based around /50 these two topics.

The traditional figures of the bride and /60 groom on the top of the cake are not required, /70 but they suggest that the top tier should hold a /80 basket of fruit, all edible. The middle tier is to /90 depict a show jumping scene and the bottom tier is /100 to be laid out as four fields, each with a /110 different crop (dash) perhaps one could show a tractor harvesting. /120

I am sure you will have fun planning the layout /130 of this cake, and Mrs Harrison looks forward to discussing /140 your designs when they are ready. **(146)**

4 Letter to Mrs Harrison confirming details

Dear Mrs Harrison

Thank you for your letter and the /10 enclosed cheque for £500 as the deposit on /20 the reception for your daughter's wedding. Also enclosed was your /30 selection of dishes for the vegetarian meal. I feel your /40 choice of soup and a hot main course is most /50 appropriate for a winter wedding.

With regard to the preparation /60 of the meal, I note your concern and I can /70 assure you that only vegetarian cheese will be used. Our /80 chef is very experienced and will follow your wishes exactly. /90

On the subject of the flowers for the bride's bouquet, /100 I think it would be a good idea if you /110 could let me have a sample of the material to /120 be used for the wedding dress to give to the /130 florist so that she may choose the most complementary colours. /140

I look forward to hearing from you soon.

Yours sincerely /150 **(150)**

5 Letter to Mrs Harrison acknowledging settlement of account

Dear Mrs Harrison

Thank you for your prompt settlement of /10 our account. I appreciate all your compliments about our service /20 and will certainly pass on your comments to all the /30 staff involved in the wedding arrangements. I must agree that /40 the day went very well from our point of view /50 and the weather was also kind to us.

It was /60 very kind of you to recommend our services to your /70 niece who is getting married next year, and I have /80 already forwarded our brochure to her outlining the services we /90 offer.

Thank you again for your kind words.

Yours sincerely /100 **(100)**

Exercise 3.1

In view of the fact that the local authority has /10 made a full inquiry at some time, I am of /^{20} the opinion that <u>preliminary enquiries</u> only should be made now. /^{30} **(30)**

Exercise 3.2

<u>In effect</u> it means that the Committee should get a /^{10} <u>second opinion</u> and I <u>have come to the conclusion</u> it /^{20} is <u>more than necessary</u> to do so <u>at this time.</u> /^{30} **(30)**

Exercise 3.3

<u>Many times</u> I've made <u>preliminary enquiries</u> about meeting someone in /^{10} <u>full authority</u> but, <u>in fact</u>, my telephone calls have been /^{20} ignored, so, <u>in my opinion</u>, <u>rather than</u> telephone again, it's /^{30} better to send a <u>letter of enquiry</u> by Recorded Delivery. /^{40} **(40)**

Exercise 3.4

From your <u>telephone enquiry</u> I understand your order is urgently /^{10} required and must be ready before the end of the /^{20} month. I am afraid it is not possible unless we /^{30} take on more staff to cope with the sudden demand. /^{40} **(40)**

Exercise 3.5

Following a <u>preliminary enquiry</u>, the social sub-committee reported to /^{10} the management committee that, <u>rather than</u> continue with the plans /^{20} to extend the sports club building, it was possible to /^{30} build a new club before the end of the year. /^{40} **(40)**

1

Dear Miss Allen

We have pleasure in enclosing your copy /^{10} of the hire agreement for the television set recently installed, /^{20} and would be grateful if you would retain this document /^{30} for future reference.

Your account number is shown on the /^{40} right-hand side of the agreement and you should quote /^{50} this on any occasion when you need to make an /^{60} enquiry in respect of your account.

Should you at any /^{70} time have any query with regard to your agreement, or /^{80} require service, a telephone call or a personal call to /^{90} the showroom will ensure prompt attention. It will assist us /^{100} considerably when service is required if you make the request /^{110} before 10 a.m. All our branches are equipped with /^{120} telephone answering machines to record messages received outside business hours /^{130} and my staff and I will be pleased to give /^{140} you any advice or assistance to enable you to get /^{150} the fullest possible enjoyment from the receiver.

For your protection, /[160] we would like to remind you that as you are /[170] responsible for the safe custody of the receiver, it will /[180] be to your own advantage to see that it is /[190] fully insured. Usually householders' comprehensive policies cover most of the /[200] risks to hired goods, but you should make sure that /[210] the sum insured is adequate to cover both this set /[220] and your own effects. If you are in doubt, your /[230] insurance broker will be able to advise you. Yours sincerely /[240] **(240)**

2

Dear Miss Allen
We now note that it is almost /[10] twelve months since you purchased a colour television receiver from /[20] us, and would like to remind you that the manufacturer's /[30] guarantee will expire on the first of next month.
We /[40] wish to draw your attention to our extended warranty in /[50] the form of a Total Cover Contract to give you /[60] peace of mind for a further three years. You will /[70] be fully covered in the event of a breakdown during /[80] the extended maintenance period, provided the goods have been in /[90] normal domestic use. Maintenance is carried out by our own /[100] fully trained service personnel and covers any repairs, both parts /[110] and labour, engineer's travelling time and workshop service if this /[120] is required.
I enclose an application form which sets out /[130] methods of payment and cost and look forward to hearing /[140] from you soon.
Yours sincerely **(145)**

3

Dear Sirs
Thank you for your recent letter.
I was /[10] encouraged to hear that your company operates an extended warranty /[20] scheme for television sets.
The most practical method of payment /[30] in my opinion is by direct debit and I therefore /[40] return the form you enclosed enabling payments to be made /[50] direct from my bank account. Yours faithfully **(57)**

4

Dear Miss Allen
Thank you for your telephone call of /[10] yesterday evening advising us that your television set needs some /[20] attention.
We note that you wish the engineer to call /[30] on Saturday and have tried to contact you several times /[40] today without success, to let you know that our engineer /[50] will be in your district on Saturday afternoon this week /[60] and will call upon you to rectify the sound fault. /[70] Yours sincerely **(72)**

5

Dear Sirs

Account No. 17/848 /^{10}

I am returning herewith this account in respect of maintenance /^{20} to my television set. Will you kindly note that in /^{30} April last I joined your three year Total Cover Contract /^{40} scheme and, as my account has been debited, can only /^{50} assume that an error has been made.

At the same /^{60} time I am still not satisfied with the sound on /^{70} the set and would appreciate another visit from the service /^{80} engineer.

Will you please cancel this account immediately and I /^{90} shall be glad to have your observations and comments. Yours /^{100} faithfully (**101**)

6

Dear Miss Allen

Examination of Television Receiver – Account No. 1 /^{10}7/848

Thank you for your letter /^{20} received today with regard to this account.

I am very /^{30} sorry indeed that an account has been issued for the /^{40} inspection and repair of your television when, in fact, the /^{50} TV is included in our Total Cover Contract. I /^{60} am, of course, arranging for the account to be withdrawn /^{70} and shall be pleased if you will accept my personal /^{80} apology for inconvenience caused on this occasion.

As you are /^{90} still not too happy with the sound on the set, /^{100} I have arranged for the engineer to call again and /^{110} make a further examination. As I believe that Saturday is /^{120} convenient for you, he will call around to see you /^{130} on Saturday morning next.

Once again, I wish to assure /^{140} you that we are always at your service.

Yours sincerely /^{150}

Philip Ames

District Manager (**154**)

Exercise 4.1

attitude	tangible	theoretical	tremendous	territory
strategy	disapproval	deadline	departure	directory
disaster	addressee			

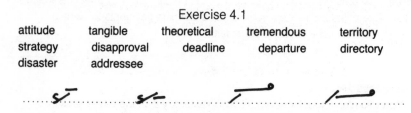

Exercise 4.2

Mrs Underwood and her husband are to undertake a transcontinental /^{10} holiday and ask for an estimate from this agency. They /^{20} wish us to arrange for translators to meet them at /^{30} various stages of their journey. It transpires

that Mr Underwood /⁴⁰ underwent a heart transplant at the end of last year /⁵⁰ and I understand that under the circumstances medical treatment may /⁶⁰ be necessary en route.
We must be careful not to /⁷⁰ undercharge for this service, but it looks as though we /⁸⁰ can still undercut our competitors. Could you transcribe the attached /⁹⁰ notes and make a detailed itinerary as soon as possible. /¹⁰⁰ **(100)**

Exercise 4.3

When played back on the video screen, the activity in /¹⁰ the town theatre recorded on the video camera showed the /²⁰ sensitivity of those taking part. **(25)**

Exercise 4.4

The gravity of the situation became apparent when the cavity /¹⁰ appeared in the wall and productivity was naturally affected immediately /²⁰ because staff were sent home. **(25)**

Exercise 4.5

Report from Managing Director to the Board of Directors. I /¹⁰ would like to introduce to you the concept of videoconferencing. /²⁰ I would describe it as linking people in different places /³⁰ by pictures and sound transmitted through telephone lines. From time /⁴⁰ to time directors and managers drive or fly off to /⁵⁰ conferences hundreds of miles away and consequently are away from /⁶⁰ the office for quite long periods of time. Other members /⁷⁰ of staff are constantly being asked to undertake the extra /⁸⁰ business activities of missing colleagues, which is usually a higher /⁹⁰ category of work than that for which they are normally /¹⁰⁰ paid. The company would have to buy the camera and /¹¹⁰ monitoring equipment, but the advantages of this system are apparent: /¹²⁰ significantly more time spent in the office and less expense /¹³⁰ in travelling costs. Conveniently, the existing conference room is perfectly /¹⁴⁰ proportioned for this facility and economically it makes sense to /¹⁵⁰ use it. **(152)**

1 Letter to an agent from a catalogue company

Dear Mrs Thompson
You will be delighted to see our /¹⁰ new Christmas Catalogue. It is full of wonderful ideas and /²⁰ extra gifts for everyone in the family as well as /³⁰ friends and neighbours. The toys and puzzles category has been /⁴⁰ extended considerably this year and includes video films and computer /⁵⁰ games, plus all the items usually advertised on the television /⁶⁰ at this time of year.
Do not underestimate your ability /⁷⁰ to sell. Point out the advantages of

buying from our /80 catalogue, such as spreading the cost over twenty weeks and /90 the pleasure and convenience of armchair shopping. Personally, I am /100 sure you will have no trouble once the customers in /110 your allotted territory see our terrific range of goods. They /120 might also like to show their friends the catalogue. Some /130 of our agents hold coffee mornings to try to increase /140 their sales at this time of the year. It is /150 a good way of making new sfriends as well.

Don't /160 forget that you are entitled to an extra cash bonus /170 if your orders total more than £1000, but /180 make sure you do not miss the deadline for delivery. /190

By the way, for every transaction made this month we /200 are donating 10p to homes for underprivileged children.

Now /210 is the perfect time to increase your sales and, of /220 course, your commission. I look forward to receiving your first /230 orders.

Yours sincerely

Trevor Bates

Catalogue Sales Manager (**238**)

2 Memo from the Sales Director to the Stationery Manager

From time to time it is decided to try to /10 improve and increase our product range, and the main area /20 targeted this season is the cards we offer in our /30 Greetings Catalogue. We already have a full range for Christmas, /40 Easter, birthdays and anniversaries, but we now propose to introduce /50 cards for other celebrations during the year, such as Valentine's /60 Day, and cards for ethnic cultures.

We need exclusive designs /70 at competitive prices so that when our customers look through /80 the catalogue for general gifts, wrappings and cards, they feel /90 absolutely compelled to order one or two of the perfectly /100 displayed new items.

I would like you to liaise with /110 the Art Supervisor on this matter and produce about a /120 dozen samples in order that we may select suitable designs. /130 I need to have these by the end of the /140 month when the next meeting is scheduled. (**147**)

3 Letter to an agent about non-payment

Dear Mrs Phillips

I would like to draw your attention /10 to the fact that we have not received any remittance /20 from you for the past six weeks. As you are /30 aware, instalments are due at the beginning of every month /40 and I must emphasise that agents are expected to be /50 prompt with their payments.

I am assuming that you have /60 overlooked this matter and suggest you send the amount owed /70 immediately. If, however, you are unable to do so for /80

any reason, please be kind enough to telephone me as /^{90} soon as possible so that I am aware of the /^{100} situation.
Yours sincerely (**103**)

4 Letter to an agent about giving up an agency because of ill health

Dear Mrs Collins
Thank you for your letter informing me /^{10} that you are unable to continue with your agency because /^{20} of ill health.
I have looked in our records and /^{30} see that you have actually been an agent with us /^{40} for the past eighteen years and have on two occasions /^{50} won prizes for outstanding sales in the Midland Region. We /^{60} very much regret having to lose you as an agent, /^{70} but as you say your illness may last for several /^{80} months or even years, we reluctantly accept your resignation.
You /^{90} say that your next-door neighbour, Mr Martin, would like /^{100} to take over your agency. As you have personally recommended /^{110} him there should not be any problem and I will /^{120} forward to him the usual forms for him to sign /^{130} and the current catalogue. I am sure you will give /^{140} Mr Martin a list of all your old customers so /^{150} that he can make an excellent start to his agency. /^{160}
Thank you for all your hard work over the years /^{170} and I would like to take this opportunity, on behalf /^{180} of the Managing Director and the Board of Directors, to /^{190} wish you good health in the future.
Yours very sincerely /^{200} (**200**)

Exercise 5.1

The <u>secretary</u> repeated the instructions to the <u>producer</u> to make /^{10} sure the necessary transport would be <u>organised</u> rapidly and the /^{20} arrangements <u>proposed</u> were beyond <u>reproach</u>. (**25**)

Exercise 5.2

It seems <u>appropriate</u> <u>at the present time</u> to send a /^{10} <u>preliminary</u> notice to announce a <u>probable</u> increase in the annual /^{20} subscription. I hope that this will meet with the <u>approval</u> /^{30} of the <u>subscribers</u> as it will result in a <u>prominent</u> /^{40} <u>improvement</u> in the <u>present</u> benefits. Subscriptions may be paid by /^{50} direct debit as before or by cheque if members <u>prefer</u>. /^{60} Cheques should be made payable to the Department of <u>Agriculture</u>. /^{70} (**70**)

Exercise 5.3

I believe <u>congratulations</u> are in order <u>at the present time</u> /^{10} as I have read in the newspaper that your essay /^{20} on <u>agriculture</u> received a certificate of approval at the preliminary /³⁰ judging. Do you feel any improvement might have been made /⁴⁰ or do you prefer it as you originally wrote it? /⁵⁰ **(50)**

1 Memo from the Manager, Pamela Green, to her staff

You will be pleased to hear that the planned move /¹⁰ into our new premises is due to take place on /²⁰ the 26th of next month.

Arrangements are being made /³⁰ for all equipment to be transferred on the previous day, /⁴⁰ Sunday, so that business will continue with as little disturbance /⁵⁰ as possible to staff, suppliers and customers.

Some weeks ago /⁶⁰ I asked for volunteers among the secretarial staff to come /⁷⁰ in on Saturday, the 24th, to get everything from /⁸⁰ their respective departments ready for the removal men on Sunday /⁹⁰ and there has been a 100 per cent response. /¹⁰⁰ Congratulations to a very loyal staff for this splendid effort. /¹¹⁰

You will find conditions in the new premises a great /¹²⁰ improvement. There is a large parking area, a shopping precinct /¹³⁰ nearby, and no longer shall we have to work in /¹⁴⁰ old over-crowded property with problem parking, but will be /¹⁵⁰ able to enjoy bright, new, open-plan offices which are /¹⁶⁰ very spacious and airy. There will be a special section /¹⁷⁰ set aside for word processing and eventually extra staff will /¹⁸⁰ be recruited for this rapidly expanding specialist part of our /¹⁹⁰ work. I have a detailed set of plans for the /²⁰⁰ new offices and intend seeing each member of staff within /²¹⁰ the next week or so to discuss appropriate work stations. /²²⁰ **(220)**

2 Letter from the Health Club to the Green Finance Company

Dear Mrs Green

We understand that your company is moving /¹⁰ premises next month and will occupy the third floor of /²⁰ this building. The Health Club is situated on the ground /³⁰ floor and we take this opportunity to welcome you and /⁴⁰ your staff to the new venue.

I am sure your /⁵⁰ staff would enjoy taking advantage of the opportunities available to /⁶⁰ them in our modern studios, perhaps at lunch breaks, after /⁷⁰ work, or even in the mornings as we open promptly /⁸⁰ at 7 a.m. We can offer toning table sessions /⁹⁰ suitable for all age groups, sunbeds and sauna, all of /¹⁰⁰ which are under the personal supervision of highly trained staff. /¹¹⁰ There is also a hair and beauty salon and a /¹²⁰ refreshment lounge. We are able to offer group membership to /¹³⁰ employees of business organisations such as your own at a /¹⁴⁰ special rate.

I enclose descriptive brochures together with details of /¹⁵⁰ the Group Schemes and look forward to hearing from you /¹⁶⁰ in due course.

Yours sincerely

Mohammed Anwar (Director) **(168)**

3 Letter from the Green Finance Company to the Health Club

Dear Mr Anwar

Thank you for your letter and kind /[10] remarks. We have now settled into the new premises, as /[20] you are no doubt aware, and several of my staff /[30] have expressed an interest in using your studios.

We are /[40] only a small company, but I am prepared to pay /[50] a Group Subscription for probably ten staff members at the /[60] present time.

First of all, though, I would appreciate having /[70] a preliminary look round before finally signing on the dotted /[80] line and committing myself. Perhaps you would give me a /[90] ring to make arrangements for this.

Yours sincerely

Pamela Green /[100] (**100**)

4 Letter to the Health Club from the Green Finance Company, enclosing cheque

Dear Mr Anwar

I was most impressed when I looked /[10] round your studios on Wednesday and have pleasure in enclosing /[20] a cheque to cover Group Membership subscriptions for ten persons. /[30] I understand membership cards will be available immediately.

Yours sincerely /[40]

Pamela Green (**42**)

Exercise 6.1

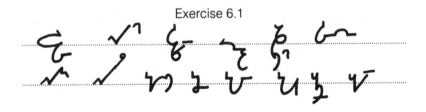

Exercise 6.2

The trade fair to be held next <u>autumn</u> is expected /[10] to be an <u>even</u> bigger event than last year. <u>Everyone</u> /[20] in the company who mans a stand will be <u>authorised</u> /[30] to park in the official car park off <u>Austin</u> Road. /[40] (**40**)

Exercise 6.3

If the <u>automation</u> of the production line is completed this /[10] <u>afternoon</u>, the Managing Director wishes to make a speech. <u>Afterwards</u> /[20] the usual monthly meeting of the Board of Directors will /[30] be held, but <u>everyone</u> else on the workforce will stay /[40] for a while to watch the components being <u>automatically</u> assembled. /[50] (**50**)

Exercise 6.4

At a conference held in an Australian academy last August, /[10] one of the speakers, Auberon Evans, asked for volunteers to /[20] evaluate his new invention which he estimated should be on /[30] the market by the end of next year. He said /[40] the evidence showed that the equipment should eventually upgrade the /[50] old standard model now produced for the automobile industry, and /[60] his company would automatically evolve as one of the leaders /[70] in the field. **(73)**

Exercise 6.5

1 I anticipate a sales demand over and above that expected.
2 The architect changed our antiquated room into a modern office.
3 Search the archives for the above-mentioned document this afternoon.
4 Our managers must always be above criticism and above suspicion.
5 Airmail letters to Austria fly in air-conditioned cargo holds.

Exercise 6.6

Lifeguards in the new ultra-modern sports centre wear matching /[10] ultra-marine costumes. Several ultra-violet sun beds are provided /[20] in an ante-room for use by club members only. /[30] **(30)**

What is uppermost in our minds is that next week /[10] we must appoint only a suitably experienced applicant with a /[20] minimum of an upper second-class degree for the vacant /[30] position on the newly extended upper storey of the building. /[40] **(40)**

Exercise 6.7

Company plans for the opening of a new shopping complex

The Mayor and Mayoress are to be asked to open /[10] the ultra-modern shopping complex in the centre of the /[20] city. Before the noon ceremony nine dignitaries will be given /[30] a reception and an audio-visual presentation on the building /[40] of the centre by the architect in one of the /[50] ante-rooms off the main lobby. Above the archway there /[60] is to be a multi-coloured banner and a white /[70] ribbon 2 inches wide suspended in front, which the Mayoress /[80] will be asked to cut. After that the Mayor will /[90] make a speech to the effect that it is an /[100] auspicious occasion and, although insignificant to the rest of the /[110] world, to our small city it is a remarkable achievement /[120] after all the years of waiting. Security will be high /[130] and police will ask for some means of identification from /[140] all the men and women who are not in the /[150] official party.

A tour of the air-conditioned centre will /[160] follow and many people may be

overawed by the <u>obvious</u> /[170] splendour of both the <u>upper storey</u> and the
ground floor. /[180] **(180)**

1 Letter from an estate agent to a client

Dear Mrs Grainger

Modern Homes is pleased to accept your /[10] instructions to sell your house at
9 Park Street.

I /[20] enclose details of our charges for the advertising and sale /[30] of your
home, together with two copies of the agreement, /[40] one of which I would like
you to sign and /[50] return to me as soon as possible. A copy of /[60] the
advertisement is also enclosed.

With regard to your query /[70] on security, any prospective purchaser should
not be able to /[80] identify the house unless they call at our office for /[90] details.
We will obviously exercise discretion as to whom we /[100] give the details, and
viewing will be strictly by appointment /[110] through ourselves. One of my staff
will accompany any client /[120] who wishes to view your property.

As you are aware, /[130] when I visited your home last night to measure the /[140]
rooms and give an estimate of the value, I noticed /[150] that the gutters needed
clearing and that two of the /[160] tiles from your roof have obviously become
loose and dislodged /[170] a few inches. These are really insignificant problems,
but I /[180] suggested that you had these faults remedied before the
advertisement /[190] is published in this week's local paper. You asked me /[200]
to recommend someone who could do this work for you /[210] and I suggested
Mr Tom Gardener, an odd-job man /[220] who regularly carries out this type of
work. I telephoned /[230] him this morning as you requested and he said he /[240]
could do the job on Thursday afternoon, if this is /[250] convenient for you. I will
assume it is unless I /[260] hear to the contrary.

Your house is a very desirable /[270] property indeed and I feel sure it will not
take /[280] very long to sell. Please let me know if I /[290] can be of further
assistance.

Yours sincerely

Paul Marsh

Partner /[300] **(300)**

2 Advertisement for the sale of a house

Modern Homes are pleased to offer for sale a truly /[10] impressive detached
family home, one of only nine of its /[20] kind. It is ideally located by the river
with extensive /[30] views to the rear, and yet is close to all /[40] local amenities
including shops, schools for all age groups, and /[50] regular transport services.
The motorway junction is just half a /[60] mile away, thereby making all main
business centres within easy /[70] reach.

This four-bedroomed property is tastefully decorated and has /[80] been maintained to the highest standard by its present owner. /^{90} It must be inspected to appreciate the charm and character /^{100} of this deceptively spacious dwelling.

The double-glazed and gas /^{110} centrally heated accommodation is very realistically priced for an early /^{120} sale. We will be very happy to discuss and arrange /^{130} a mortgage on this property. To view the house and /^{140} for further details, contact the selling agents, Modern Homes. **(149)**

3 Letter from an estate agent to a client confirming an offer to buy

Dear Mrs Grainger

I am very pleased to inform you /^{10} that we have today received a firm offer for your /^{20} house from Ms Annette Hudson, a business woman who has /^{30} been promoted in her job and consequently must move into /^{40} this area to open a new branch for her company. /^{50} She has viewed several properties and considers that the features /^{60} of your house are over and above the rest with /^{70} regard to design, position and interior decoration.

Ms Hudson, therefore, /^{80} is prepared to pay the asking price to secure the /^{90} house. However, she insists that she must buy the property /^{100} freehold and I suggest that you get in touch with /^{110} your solicitor immediately to see if this is possible because, /^{120} as you are aware, at the moment the house is /^{130} leasehold.

Ms Hudson is also offering to pay the sum /^{140} of £1000 to include the high-quality carpets /^{150} and matching curtains in all rooms and the blinds in /^{160} the bathroom, kitchen and laundry. This figure is also to /^{170} include the television aerial which is situated in the loft. /^{180} She has asked whether you are prepared to sell her /^{190} the unusual wall light fittings in the lounge, and perhaps /^{200} you could suggest a reasonable price if you are prepared /^{210} to leave them.

Ms Hudson has sold her house in /^{220} Liverpool and contracts have already been exchanged. The building society /^{230} has guaranteed Ms Hudson a mortgage and it is obvious /^{240} that she is eager to complete on your property as /^{250} soon as possible. As you have already bought your own /^{260} new home, I feel everything should go through quite quickly, /^{270} probably by the end of next month, which I hope /^{280} would be ideal for you.

I look forward to hearing /^{290} your comments.

Yours sincerely **(294)**

Exercise 7.1

Dear Sirs

In reply to your letter, we regret to /^{10} inform you that although we have a large number of /²⁰ chrome taps in stock, we are <u>out of stock</u> of /³⁰ brass taps and have been <u>unable to obtain</u> further supplies. /⁴⁰

Assuring you of our <u>prompt attention</u> at all times.

Yours /⁵⁰ **(50)**

Exercise 7.2

Dear Madam

<u>We have received your letter</u> today and we /¹⁰ wish to say <u>we were sorry</u> you were not notified /²⁰ of our <u>change of address</u>. If you return the goods /³⁰ <u>at your earliest convenience</u> to the address now shown, the /⁴⁰ matter of repayment will be attended to immediately.

Yours faithfully /⁵⁰ **(50)**

1 A circular letter – recipients' names will be inserted later

Dear

No doubt you will remember just how quickly we /¹⁰ were reminded very early last year of the perils of /²⁰ winter. Here at Home and Away Motors, we are taking /³⁰ this opportunity of offering you added winter protection for your /⁴⁰ vehicle, which is fully backed by the vehicle manufacturer. We /⁵⁰ are pleased to tell you that by paying out what /⁶⁰ we consider a very reasonable amount of money, you can /⁷⁰ be assured that your car will receive a complete winter /⁸⁰ warranty service. This guarantees that under the warranty if any /⁹⁰ repaired or checked component fails within 12 000 miles or /¹⁰⁰ before 30 April next year all the work which may /¹¹⁰ be required will be carried out completely free of charge. /¹²⁰

I am enclosing a leaflet giving further details, together with /¹³⁰ the price list appropriate to your vehicle. Also, for the /¹⁴⁰ first sixty bookings a superb first aid kit will be /¹⁵⁰ given for you to keep in the car.

Why not /¹⁶⁰ telephone our service reception today and ask for Trevor or /¹⁷⁰ Mandy?

Yours sincerely **(173)**

2 A reply to a customer who is requesting information. The letter contains three numbered points

Dear Mrs Greaves

We have received your letter of 20 /¹⁰ September. It was a pleasure to hear from you again /²⁰ and to know that you are considering taking your car /³⁰ to France when you go on holiday in the early /⁴⁰ spring.

Despite your fears, I don't think you need have /⁵⁰ any worries about driving on the right hand side of /⁶⁰ the road, particularly as your friend will navigate and you /⁷⁰ are having another rear view mirror fitted on the passenger /⁸⁰ side. I must stress that overtaking might be a little /⁹⁰ difficult, but will become easier as you become familiar with /^{100} the situation. Don't forget that road distances and speeds are /^{110} given in kilometres, so I suggest a prior check on /^{120} the conversions if you are not fully conversant with them. /^{130}

It is essential to make a booking on the ferry /^{140} as soon as possible because these get very busy especially /^{150} at weekends.

In response to your queries:

1 Yes, we /^{160} can supply and fit headlight converters and also the yellow /^{170} tinted headlight covers.

2 You do need a letter plate /^{180} bearing the GB sign for travel abroad.

3 I /^{190} enclose a leaflet about travel insurance cover, not only for /^{200} the vehicle but also for yourself and your passenger. There /^{210} is also the matter of the green card which is /^{220} needed to ensure full protection on your insurance cover.

I /^{230} know I am preaching to the converted when I say /^{240} that your car should be in tip-top condition before /^{250} embarking on the trip and it seems almost unnecessary to /^{260} remind you to book in for a full service shortly /^{270} before your departure date.

I do hope you have a /^{280} pleasant time and this letter has helped to allay your /^{290} doubts. Quite frankly, with the driving experience you have had /^{300} over the years, I can't see any problems developing.

Remember /^{310} me to your brother. I do not seem to have /^{320} seen him at the Badminton Club lately.

Yours sincerely (**329**)

3 Memorandum to forecourt staff

I have just been reading a report from the Trading /^{10} Standards Service who have been checking tyre pressure gauges for /^{20} public use on garage forecourts. Of 29/^{30}5 gauges checked on garage forecourts, 24 per cent /^{40} gave inaccurate readings. This failure rate is abysmal.

We are /^{50} all aware that incorrectly inflated tyres create a serious safety /^{60} hazard together with legal implications for drivers.

Will you please /^{70} make doubly sure that our own gauges do not fall /^{80} into the heavy failure category by making constant checks to /^{90} see that they are correctly correlated and maintained. (**98**)

4 Letter of invitation

Dear Mr Stead

As one of our long-standing customers /^{10} I am pleased to invite you to be our guest /^{20} at a special preview evening on Thursday 12 October from /^{30} 6 p.m. onwards to mark the arrival of our /^{40} latest model.

I do hope you will be able to /^{50} join us for what promises to be an enjoyable evening /^{60} with cheese and wine, when you will be able to /^{70} see the new model for yourself before it is shown /⁸⁰ to the general public. To stress our awareness of the /⁹⁰ foolishness of drinking and driving, the wines chosen are from /¹⁰⁰ a specially selected range of non-alcoholic wines almost indistinguishable /¹¹⁰ from the vintage article. Do please bring your partner along /¹²⁰ (dash) there will be lots for everyone to see and /¹³⁰ do and food for all.

The model represents excellent value /¹⁴⁰ for money, combining distinctive styling with the highest quality engineering /¹⁵⁰ that you have come to expect from such a large /¹⁶⁰ manufacturing group.

Please confirm your acceptance of my request by /¹⁷⁰ completing the invitation card enclosed. I look forward to seeing /¹⁸⁰ you on the 12th.

Yours sincerely

General Manager **(188)**

5 Memo to Miss Dean, General Office

I attach a leaflet which gives details of /¹⁰ word processing courses at Head Office. Is there anyone you /²⁰ wish to nominate for one of these? Please make sure /³⁰ there will be no clash with late holidays. **(38)**

Exercise 8.1

camera   free   committee   spaghetti   potato   memo
true

Exercise 8.2

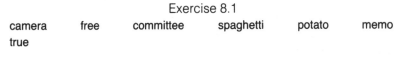

Exercise 8.3

There will be a buffet at the Quay Cafe next /¹⁰ week to celebrate Troy's forty years of employment in the /²⁰ business. He is a model employee, always obeys company policy, /³⁰ and never gets annoyed with his members of staff. We /⁴⁰ will present him with a suitable gift and give a /⁵⁰ bouquet to his wife. It should be a joyous occasion. /⁶⁰ **(60)**

Exercise 8.4

I am writing to you regarding the curtains belonging to /¹⁰ me which I collected from your young assistant at the /²⁰ dry cleaning shop after they had been lengthened. When I /³⁰ went to hang the curtains up, I discovered a triangular /⁴⁰ shaped hole along the seam. I will be bringing back /⁵⁰ the damaged item for a satisfactory repair on Wednesday evening. /⁶⁰ **(60)**

Exercise 8.5

Dear Mrs Monk
I wish to order twenty chunky sweaters /¹⁰ in pink. I think that the donkey and

monkey designs /²⁰ on the front are quite delightful. I know that your /³⁰ business is ranked highly amongst similar companies and I accept /⁴⁰ your assurance that these goods will not shrink. Many thanks /⁵⁰ for the prompt delivery of my last order.
Yours sincerely /⁶⁰ **(60)**

Exercise 8.6

1 The Managing Director concealed his irritability when members of the Board of Directors agreed he was unreasonable in this case. **(20)**
2 It is your responsibility to ensure that computers are available only to authorised staff or valuable data may be destroyed. **(20)**
3 It would be sensible to check the compatibility of the software before you buy or you will be personally accountable. **(20)**
4 The office rebel was in trouble with the manager when he filled the drawers with soap bubbles for a prank. **(20)**

Exercise 8.7

The successful takeover bid of the pharmaceutical company meant that /¹⁰ the zoology and biology departments had to be closed. The /²⁰ biologists were made redundant, the zoologists were transferred. The company /³⁰ psychologist reported that it was very bad for staff morale. /⁴⁰ **(40)**

Exercise 8.8
Courses offered at a college

Evening classes at the College start again in September. Some /¹⁰ years ago the number of courses we offered was very /²⁰ limited, but a few weeks ago we decided that this /³⁰ year we would have more classes on offer (dash) word /⁴⁰ processing, Hindi, woodwork, sociology and psychology. If you have an /⁵⁰ inability to read and write and think it is an /⁶⁰ insuperable problem, we offer confidential adult literacy classes in absolute /⁷⁰ privacy. A new short course this year is tree surgery /⁸⁰ and anyone interested will learn the safe and correct way /⁹⁰ of cutting a bough from a tree. In fact, it /¹⁰⁰ is almost impossible not to find a course to suit /¹¹⁰ everyone and, all things being equal, every student benefits from /¹²⁰ attending. Absolutely no qualifications are required. Students must be 16 /¹³⁰ years of age and are responsible for buying their own /¹⁴⁰ books and materials. **(143)**

1 Letter to a prospective customer

Dear Mrs King
In reply to your telephone enquiry yesterday, /¹⁰ I am pleased to send you our colour brochure giving /²⁰ full details of our health spa, and reservation form and /³⁰ tariff. The purpose-built mansion was built four years ago /⁴⁰ to a very

high specification, and has been tastefully decorated /⁵⁰ to our own requirements. Each of the forty bedrooms is /⁶⁰ individually designed and luxuriously appointed with en suite facilities. The /⁷⁰ extensive walled grounds are especially landscaped to ensure complete privacy /⁸⁰ for our guests and are stocked with many unusual trees, /⁹⁰ shrubs, aromatic plants and flowers. Guests may enjoy strolling through /¹⁰⁰ the gardens or may participate in the many outdoor activities /¹¹⁰ we have available, such as tennis, croquet and bowling.

Health, /¹²⁰ beauty and fitness are our specialisms and each of our /¹³⁰ consultants is a highly trained expert in his or her /¹⁴⁰ own field. Our reception and support staff are very friendly, /¹⁵⁰ willing and helpful.

Everything is here for the revitalisation programme /¹⁶⁰ you need. We have gone to great lengths to provide /¹⁷⁰ the kind of facilities our guests require, together with a /¹⁸⁰ relaxing, soothing atmosphere.

I am sure that when you have /¹⁹⁰ studied the literature you will wish to spend some time /²⁰⁰ here with us and I look forward to receiving your /²¹⁰ firm booking.

Yours sincerely

Janice Bradbury

Bradbury Health Spa (**219**)

2 Letter confirming a booking

Dear Mrs King

We have just received your fax booking /¹⁰ for one week commencing 27 January, and are pleased /²⁰ to confirm that the Blue Bedroom you requested is available. /³⁰ As you have no transport of your own, it is /⁴⁰ no problem at all for me to arrange for our /⁵⁰ chauffeur to collect you from the station when the London /⁶⁰ train arrives.

On your arrival, one of our consultants will /⁷⁰ discuss your requirements with you and thereafter will prepare an /⁸⁰ individual and itemised schedule for you for the entire week. /⁹⁰ I understand that you wish to partake in daily aerobic /¹⁰⁰ classes and use the equipment in the gym throughout your /¹¹⁰ stay. I am pleased to inform you that these are /¹²⁰ available without extra charge.

If you have any further individual /¹³⁰ requirements please let me know. Let me assure you that /¹⁴⁰ the staff here will do everything possible to make your /¹⁵⁰ stay enjoyable.

Yours sincerely

Janice Bradbury

Bradbury Health Spa (**159**)

3 A letter to Mrs King about a group booking

Dear Mrs King

Thank you for your kind letter saying /¹⁰ that you enjoyed your stay here so much and made /²⁰ some new friends. It was interesting to hear that when /³⁰ you returned to work everyone in the office thought you /⁴⁰ looked well and radiant after your week with us, and /⁵⁰ your colleagues would now all like to come along for /⁶⁰ one of our 'Head to Toe' days. As you will /⁷⁰ have read in our brochure, this includes aquatherapy, body massage, /⁸⁰ manicure, pedicure and facial treatments. We have make-up to /⁹⁰ suit all ethnic skin types.

I have checked the reservations /¹⁰⁰ for the dates you suggested, and unfortunately 4 February is /¹¹⁰ fully booked, but 15 March is still available. I have /¹²⁰ pencilled in your party of ten people and would be /¹³⁰ grateful if you could confirm the booking as soon as /¹⁴⁰ possible. Regrettably, I am unable to offer a discount for /¹⁵⁰ group bookings because all our treatments are individually prepared for /¹⁶⁰ each client.

I look forward to hearing from you.

Yours /¹⁷⁰ sincerely (**171**)

Exercise 9.1

1 To be <u>independent</u> is <u>hardly</u> the same as being <u>indispensable</u>. (**10**)
2 There was no <u>evidence</u> two years ago that the slump in the textile <u>industries</u> in <u>England</u> would come as <u>quickly</u> and <u>suddenly</u> as it did. (**25**)
3 <u>Unfortunately</u> we were at a <u>disadvantage</u> because although we were sure there was no <u>indication</u> that the machinery had not been <u>correctly</u> fitted the <u>Industrial</u> Injuries Board did not agree. (**30**)

Exercise 9.2

Recently that manufacturing company <u>unfortunately</u> went into liquidation after <u>substantially</u> /¹⁰ losing business. <u>Formerly</u>, it was <u>closely</u> connected to an industry /²⁰ which <u>evidently</u> went <u>rapidly</u> into decline and <u>clearly</u> it would /³⁰ <u>eventually</u> have to close. <u>Apparently</u>, all the workers quickly obtained /⁴⁰ new jobs when another factory <u>conveniently</u> and <u>quickly</u> opened nearby. /⁵⁰ (**50**)

Exercise 9.3

<u>Constantly</u> I have to inform all callers that they need /¹⁰ an appointment and cannot <u>instantly</u> see my boss. One agent /²⁰ <u>consistently</u> arrives promptly every Monday morning and <u>persistently</u> tries to /³⁰ persuade me to let him in. <u>Consequently</u>, I tell him /⁴⁰ my boss is out which, <u>incidentally</u>, is usually the truth. /⁵⁰ (**50**)

Exercise 9.4

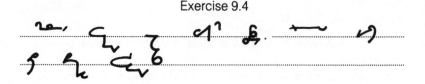

Exercise 9.5

1 A <u>preliminary enquiry established</u> that the accident had been <u>unavoidable</u>.
   (10)

2 <u>Today</u> I am going <u>to do</u> some painting as I am feeling <u>industrious</u> and
   <u>consequently</u> making <u>arrangements</u> to start <u>instantly</u>. **(20)**

3 <u>Down the</u> road <u>between the</u> park and the river is the Village Hall and, as
   some rooms are <u>unoccupied</u> at present, it is an <u>alternative</u> place to <u>arrange</u>
   the <u>entertainment</u>. **(30)**

1 Memo from Personnel Officer to Social Club Secretary

JIM

When the next issue of the staff newspaper is /[10] being prepared, I shall be
glad if the attached letter /[20] could be included. This is all part of the drive /[30]
we are having towards conserving the world's resources.

YASMIN **(39)**

2 Circular letter accompanying the memo above

Dear Colleagues

You are no doubt all aware that we /[10] should be concerned about our
environment and the danger the /[20] greenhouse effect is having on our planet
as more and /[30] more of nature's bounties are being used up and wasted. /[40]
The management feels that this company and its subsidiary industries /[50]
ought to be playing their part in preserving the world /[60] we live in for our
children and grandchildren. We would, /[70] therefore, welcome suggestions
from any of the workforce about methods /[80] we can employ to do our bit
towards recycling or /[90] simply making the factory grounds a more attractive
place.

Gift /[100] vouchers will be presented to the three employees who come /[110] up
with the best and most workable ideas. We have /[120] already ordered waste
bins for the car parks as a /[130] first step towards reducing litter.

Yours sincerely

Yasmin Kalil **(139)**

3 A notice following on from the letter and memo. It contains three numbered points

Environment Competition

The following three suggestions were judged to be /[10] the best and Ali Bashir
from Marketing, Sandra Booth from /[20] the Storeroom, and Tom Parry from
the Machine Shop have /[30] each been given Gift Vouchers worth £30.

1 A /[40] large container will be placed between the two car parks /[50] for
   depositing empty juice, beer or pop cans. This will /[60] be divided down the
   middle to keep steel and aluminium /[70] cans separate.

Not only will this reduce the amount tipped /[80] into landfill sites, but it will also take 95 /[90] per cent less energy to produce aluminium from recycled materials /[100] than from using raw materials.

2 The spare ground behind /[110] the dining block will be turned into a wild garden /[120] by being seeded with wild flowers and ornamental grasses to /[130] encourage birds, bees and butterflies, and also to be pleasing /[140] to the eye when the flowers are in bloom.

3 /[150] Car stickers will be produced and made available to the /[160] workforce to encourage others to become aware of conservation (dash) /[170] perhaps bearing a reminder about using 'green' petrol.

Thank you /[180] to all entrants for your interest.

Yasmin Kalil

Personnel Officer /[190] (**190**)

Exercise 10.1

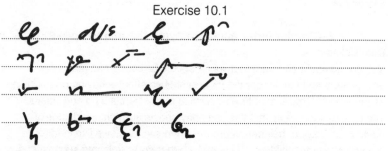

Exercise 10.2

The sales office has been <u>pleasantly</u> extended and <u>luxuriously</u> refurbished. /[10] Please <u>refrain</u> from smoking. New <u>fixtures</u> have been bought for /[20] the <u>publicity</u> literature and an espresso coffee machine and <u>refrigerator</u> /[30] have been installed for those <u>people</u> working in the department. /[40] (**40**)

Exercise 10.3

1 I was overwhelmed by <u>cheerfulness</u> and <u>joyfulness</u> when I received the letter inviting me to attend for an interview tomorrow. (**20**)

2 The <u>usefulness</u> of the new diary software is especially suitable for me when working because of my constant <u>forgetfulness</u> and in the <u>fullness</u> of time it will pay for itself. (**30**)

Exercise 10.4

1 We must take great care to avoid all accidents in the factory which might be caused by <u>carelessness</u> and <u>thoughtlessness</u>. (**20**)

2 We must fight the <u>callousness</u> of our competitors with <u>fearlessness</u> if we are to sustain and improve our market share. (**20**)

Exercise 10.5

When you first look for a job you hope to $/^{10}$ exchange your life in college for one in employment. First $/^{20}$ of all you must produce multiple copies of your C/^{30}V and send one with every application you make. You $/^{40}$ may get frequent interviews and be faced with unexpected questions, $/^{50}$ but it is unfortunate that your inexperience will usually mean $/^{60}$ that you are not successful straight away. When you are $/^{70}$ offered a job, look as far as possible into the $/^{80}$ pension arrangements because very few people want to stay in $/^{90}$ the same job for ever and ever. **(97)**

1 Letter to a new employee

Dear Mr Cox

First of all, I am pleased to $/^{10}$ confirm that we are offering you the position of Export $/^{20}$ Sales Executive with this company, based in Oxford. The Board $/^{30}$ was particularly impressed with your fluent knowledge of French and $/^{40}$ Spanish and expressed the opinion that your application was outstanding. $/^{50}$ You will be working within the framework outlined at your $/^{60}$ interview and will be personally involved in expanding our European $/^{70}$ sales, which unfortunately have not increased recently due mainly to $/^{80}$ inflation and the unexpected expulsion of one of our sales $/^{90}$ team. You will be expected to make frequent visits to $/^{100}$ Paris and Madrid as you will be responsible for the $/^{110}$ employment and training of inexperienced local agents in our multiple $/^{120}$ outlets. You will also prepare the foreign language versions of $/^{130}$ our product leaflets for the European Community.

I am sure $/^{140}$ you will enjoy the freedom and flexibility of this position. $/^{150}$ May I express the hope that you will be very $/^{160}$ happy working with this company.

Yours sincerely

Rex Baxter

Personnel $/^{170}$ Officer **(171)**

2 Memo to Works Manager

Health and Safety

It is time to review our existing $/^{10}$ policy document on Health and Safety. Revision is necessary as $/^{20}$ the nature of the work carried out in the factory $/^{30}$ has altered and new plant has been introduced into the $/^{40}$ workplace. There have also been considerable changes in the personnel $/^{50}$ who are inexperienced in our safety routines and the care $/^{60}$ of toxic materials.

With particular reference to explosions and fire $/^{70}$ hazards, I attach a list of items to be considered $/^{80}$ from which the final details will be extricated. I suggest $/^{90}$ that we hold a meeting with all departmental managers and $/^{100}$

safety representatives next Friday in the Pavilion Room in order /^{110} to consider the various points, exchange views and extract ideas /^{120} from all who attend. I would like all accidents linked /^{130} to work to be studied to see if more training /^{140} or better safeguards are required. As far as possible we /^{150} must implement more frequent safety checks. I am convinced of /^{160} the usefulness of such exercises.

The new statement is to /^{170} be produced in leaflet form and a copy enclosed with /^{180} each employee's pay slip at the end of the month. /^{190} **(190)**

3 Notice from Personnel Manager to all staff

Annual Appraisals

Next week is the time for the formal /^{10} annual appraisal of all staff. Let me explain, for the /^{20} benefit of new employees who are inexperienced in this procedure, /^{30} that this will take the form of an interview for /^{40} approximately half an hour with your supervisor or head of /^{50} department.

I would like to remind everyone of the purpose /^{60} of appraisals. First of all, they give us the chance /^{70} to reflect on the past performance of the employee and /^{80} review the job description. Problems involving any aspect of work /^{90} may be discussed and it may be that we could /^{100} discover training needs within the company. As far as possible /^{110} we hope to conduct these interviews with carefulness and we /^{120} hope to assess potential for promotion for those who do /^{130} not wish to stay in the same job for ever /^{140} and ever. This is a good time to extricate ideas /^{150} and opinions and should not be seen as an invasion /^{160} of privacy or a time for callousness. We feel it /^{170} is important for everyone to be happy in their employment. /^{180}

A confidential report on every employee is prepared for the /^{190} personnel records and a copy is given to the individual /^{200} concerned. **(201)**

4 Memo to all office staff

It has been decided that from the first of next /^{10} month we will move away from the standard 9 a. /^{20}m. to 5 p.m. working day to a system /^{30} of flexitime. The principle of the system is that staff /^{40} may choose the hours they work as long as they /^{50} are present during 'core' times and work the mandatory number /^{60} of hours per month. Core times are from 10 a. /^{70}m. until noon and 2 p.m. until 4 p. /^{80}m.

Staff relying on public transport may, therefore, come to /^{90} work and leave earlier or later, depending on the times /^{100} of their trains or buses. There are also obvious benefits /^{110} for people who use their own cars to come to /^{120} work, as they can avoid the rush hour traffic. Staff /^{130} may accumulate additional time worked in order to have an /^{140} extra day off.

I attach a time sheet which must /^{150} be completed each month by every member of staff and /^{160} be signed and checked by their immediate superior before passing /^{170} it to the Personnel Department for our records. **(178)**

Exercise 11.1
Speed drive on letter L – notice which form of L is used
The girl climbed the long hill, located the cliff ledge /^{10} and lazily looked at the clear landscape below. It all /^{20} looked unfamiliar from this angle and the looming black clouds /^{30} growing larger and larger behind the railway lines clothed it /^{40} in a yellow light. Rarely had she seen such a /^{50} lovely view and luckily her camera was full of film. /^{60} **(60)**

Exercise 11.2
Speed drive on letter M

Dear Mrs Dingmar
As one of our special customers we /^{10} take this opportunity to remind you of our mammoth summer /^{20} sale which begins on Monday morning next in our bargain /^{30} basement. More and more customers rely on our judgement in /^{40} offering them the best value for money.
You may be /^{50} assured of our immediate attention at all times.
Yours sincerely /^{60} **(60)**

Exercise 11.3
Speed drive on letter W
In most parts of the world, workers enjoy a weekend /^{10} break. In cooler climates if the weather is warm, work /^{20}-a day worries are forgotten as people enjoy motoring, walking, /^{30} swimming or just relaxing in the garden depending on what /^{40} they consider priorities. Leisure periods must cover all eventualities because /^{50} all work and no play makes Jack a dull boy. /^{60} **(60)**

Exercise 11.4
Practice sentences
(a) The magnolias were truly magnificent and attracted country-wide attention. **(10)**
(b) Priority was given to the most senior members of staff in the multi-storey car park on an experimental basis. **(20)**
(c) Ladies and Gentlemen
    I would like the Governor to see the documents which have been submitted, before the ambassador arrives. **(20)**
(d) A retired member of staff gave a vote of thanks, as a matter of course, following the manager's remarks about the new urban motorway development. **(25)**
(e) Dear Mr and Mrs Miller

By all means contact the authorities about the legality of the development. Best of luck in your efforts. Yours sincerely (25)

1 Letter from the Managing Director of a travel agency that is hoping to attract more customers

Dear Traveller

I would like to introduce you to my /¹⁰ company, Aqua Travel, although this introduction might not be strictly /²⁰ necessary as we are one of the premier cruise specialists /³⁰ in the country.

We can offer you some very special /⁴⁰ brand new cruises for next year on even the busiest /⁵⁰ sailing dates together with an exclusive introductory discount on the /⁶⁰ ones listed below. Our Sales and Marketing Department Manager will /⁷⁰ be delighted to answer any questions you may have arising /⁸⁰ from these preliminary details (colon)

10-day Winter Sun Cruises /⁹⁰ from Southampton, calling at certain ports in Spain, Portugal, Gibraltar /¹⁰⁰ and Majorca with time ashore. As an early booking bonus, /¹¹⁰ this cruise has the benefit of free personal insurance and /¹²⁰ free transport to the docks from most major towns and /¹³⁰ cities in the country.

20-night Fly Cruise holiday to /¹⁴⁰ Antarctica, sailing from Argentina and calling in at the Falkland /¹⁵⁰ Islands followed by cruising through the Antarctic amid a stunning /¹⁶⁰ landscape of glaciers and rugged mountain peaks. The opportunity to /¹⁷⁰ see wildlife unique to this part of the world should /¹⁸⁰ not be missed. This cruise is from 6 to 2 /¹⁹⁰5 January next during the southern summer when temperatures are /²⁰⁰ moderate and the sun rarely sets. A 5 per cent /²¹⁰ early booking discount will be given.

We look forward to /²²⁰ hearing from you and assure you of our prompt attention /²³⁰ at all times. A price list, together with other present /²⁴⁰ availabilities, is enclosed.

Yours faithfully (245)

2 Letter from Mr Stephen Naylor to the Sales and Marketing Manager of Aqua Travel, Short Street, Cambridge

Dear Sir

In reply to your circular letter we were /¹⁰ interested to read of the new cruise to Antarctica. Whilst /²⁰ this is something we would very much like to do, /³⁰ we feel it is a little too expensive for my /⁴⁰ wife and I to contemplate at the present time. We /⁵⁰ have a large mortgage and my wife no longer works /⁶⁰ while the children are young, but we do, however, have /⁷⁰ an insurance policy due to mature shortly and we are /⁸⁰ anxious to have a similar type of holiday on the /⁹⁰ strength of this. We would, therefore, appreciate details of any /¹⁰⁰

cruises you may have which sail up the coast of /[110] Norway and into the Arctic Circle. It would appear that /[120] June is the best time of year to do this /[130] cruise and so visit the Land of the Midnight Sun /[140] in all its splendour.
I shall be pleased to hear /[150] from you at your earliest convenience.
Yours faithfully (**158**)

3 Reply to Mr and Mrs Naylor from Aqua Travel

Dear Mr and Mrs Naylor
Thank you very much for /[10] your letter received today. I have much pleasure in enclosing /[20] details of the two cruises we operate which sail through /[30] Norwegian waters. A separate price list is enclosed.
Cruise 1 /[40] is a 14-day cruise departing from Tilbury. You will /[50] see that this voyage, in addition to cruising the Norwegian /[60] coast, returns via Iceland.
Cruise 2 is a 7-day /[70] trip sailing from and returning to Bergen with connecting flights /[80] from Newcastle upon Tyne included in the price.
On both /[90] cruises shore excursions are carefully chosen to make the most /[100] of every moment ashore and the ships themselves are floating /[110] first-class hotels. They represent the last word in luxury /[120] living.
I look forward to receiving your completed reservation form /[130] and assure you of a holiday to remember whichever journey /[140] you decide to make.
Yours sincerely
Sales and Marketing Manager /[150] (**150**)

4 Confirmation of booking

Dear Sir
Thank you for your letter and details of /[10] cruises to Norway. Cruise 2 seems to meet our requirements /[20] perfectly and I would like to make a firm booking /[30] for 8 June.
I enclose a cheque for one hundred /[40] pounds as deposit on the holiday plus the full cost /[50] of the travel insurance. Please confirm safe receipt of this /[60] and send me the detailed itinerary at your earliest convenience. /[70] Many thanks.
Yours faithfully (**74**)

5 Cancellation of booking

Dear Sir
7 DAY CRUISE TO NORWAY – BOOKING NO J /[10] 541
With regard to the booking on the /[20] above cruise on 8 June, I regret to inform you /[30] that because my husband was involved in an accident at /[40] work last week, I am afraid we shall have to /[50] cancel this holiday. He is at

present in hospital with /⁶⁰ two broken legs and the doctors say he will be /⁷⁰ unable to travel abroad for at least six months.

As /⁸⁰ we took out the travel insurance recommended by your firm, /⁹⁰ will you please look into the possibility of a refund /¹⁰⁰ and let me know the appropriate procedure as soon as /¹¹⁰ possible.

Naturally we are extremely disappointed, but if all goes /¹²⁰ well we hope to be able to make another booking /¹³⁰ when my husband has fully recovered.

Yours faithfully

Margaret Naylor /¹⁴⁰ (**140**)

Exercise 12.1

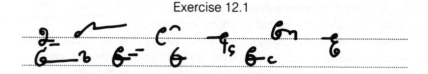

Exercise 12.2

There will be a meeting on Thursday afternoon to discuss /¹⁰ my proposals to increase our profit margins and gain new /²⁰ customers. I will disclose these to you with the aid /³⁰ of several illustrations. Thousands of pounds were lost last year /⁴⁰ through an administrative discrepancy and unless something is done as /⁵⁰ soon as possible, our previously successful transport business will suffer. /⁶⁰ I am also keen to start a scheme to save /⁷⁰ wasted resources and it is essential that a suitable solution /⁸⁰ is found to these problems. (**85**)

Exercise 12.3

1 That high street jeweller was successfully importing superfine semi-precious stones and then setting them in silver rings and bracelets. (**20**)
2 The young supervisor of the building firm won a prize for his semi-circular layout of the semi-detached homes. (**20**)

Exercise 12.4

A self-defence course for employees, which is being run /¹⁰ by the supervisor himself, starts next week. These classes aim /²⁰ to make the participants more self-confident and self-assured. /³⁰ (**30**)

Exercise 12.5

Most of the successful businesses possess a computer. Self-employed /¹⁰ people who know nothing about computers should resist the temptation /²⁰ to set up their own <u>system</u> because <u>this is</u> a /³⁰ <u>superb</u> formula for economic <u>disaster</u>. They should get professional <u>assistance,</u> /⁴⁰ and once their <u>purchases</u> of software and hardware have been /⁵⁰ installed on the <u>premises</u> the <u>emphasis</u> must be on security. /⁶⁰ <u>Access</u> should be denied to anyone who is not authorised. /⁷⁰ **(70)**

1 Memo to the Training Manager from the Managing Director about making a video

After our preliminary meeting last week about making a sales /¹⁰ video, I have been making some enquiries and it appears /²⁰ that the most experienced company doing this work is Business /³⁰ Videos.

I have been in touch with Mr Brian Stevens /⁴⁰ and he is coming to see us next Wednesday at /⁵⁰ 1400 hours to discuss our requirements. Obviously, he will /⁶⁰ be given a tour of the premises to see our /⁷⁰ facilities and decide the best way to promote our software /⁸⁰ training company and give emphasis to our various services.

During /⁹⁰ the recording, Business Videos would prefer access to all of /¹⁰⁰ our training rooms in order to compile a superb film. /¹¹⁰ Unfortunately, some of our rooms may be unoccupied during that /¹²⁰ time, so it may mean careful rescheduling of some of /¹³⁰ our groups.

Mr Stevens suggested that we have a famous /¹⁴⁰ personality to play a prominent part in the production and /¹⁵⁰ to enhance our corporate image, because market research has proved /¹⁶⁰ that this is very successful.

Please give this matter some /¹⁷⁰ thought and let me know your views before the meeting. /¹⁸⁰ **(180)**

2 Letter to Brian Stevens, Business Videos

Dear Brian

I was delighted to receive the preview copy /¹⁰ of our new promotional video. My staff and I watched /²⁰ it this afternoon and feel that it illustrates perfectly our /³⁰ product, with an appropriate emphasis on quality of service.

I /⁴⁰ propose to send copies of the video to all the /⁵⁰ large companies within a 15 mile radius to see what /⁶⁰ effect this has. Could you therefore arrange for twenty copies /⁷⁰ to be produced and sent to me as soon as /⁸⁰ possible? Thank you again for making a superb and, I /⁹⁰ hope, successful video.

Yours sincerely **(95)**

3 Memo from the Managing Director to the Training Manager

You may be amazed to hear that we have had /¹⁰ over one hundred replies from our advertisement for a Training /²⁰ Officer. I believe that our new sales video which we /³⁰ have recently distributed has drawn considerable attention to our company /^{40} and perhaps this is the reason for such a good /^{50} response.

After much deliberation I have managed to come up /^{60} with a short list of five people for interview and /^{70} photocopies of their applications and CVs are attached.

I /^{80} suggest we plan the interview for Tuesday, 12 November. I /^{90} think we need to set aside a whole day for /^{100} this, as I am asking each interviewee to prepare a /^{110} short demonstration and talk on a software package of his /^{120} or her choice. As we have discovered before, it is /^{130} not always the most qualified person who is the best /^{140} at portraying the sort of image we require; dedication and /^{150} enthusiasm are preferable.

I have asked the Restaurant Manager to /^{160} prepare a buffet for 1230 hours in the Board /^{170} Room and I think we should offer just coffee, tea /^{180} or soft drinks because these people are travelling from all /^{190} parts of the country and will need to drive back /^{200} in the evening.

I am also enclosing the agenda for /^{210} the interview day. (**213**)

4 Letter from the Training Manager to a prospective client
Dear Sir

I am sure our name is familiar to /^{10} you as being one of the country's largest training companies /^{20} specialising in various types of software. Many companies like yours /^{30} frequently install new or upgraded software and this poses a /^{40} problem to the management on how to train staff.

This /^{50} company can solve the problem. We can teach your employees /^{60} any commercial software package currently on the market (dash) whether /^{70} it is word processing, accounts, stock control, spreadsheet or database. /^{80} Training may be carried out in our superbly equipped centre /^{90} or on your own premises if this is the method /^{100} you prefer. Every course is tailor-made to your individual /^{110} requirements.

When you have watched our promotional video enclosed with /^{120} this letter, I am sure you will appreciate that, on /^{130} analysis, our service is cost effective. As Training Manager I /^{140} am available for consultation and will be pleased to make /^{150} an appointment to discuss your needs.

Yours faithfully (**158**)

Exercise 13.1
A cash injection from capital reserves will be necessary if /^{10} our application is not to be rejected by the bank. /^{20} (**20**)

Exercise 13.2
The photographer rejected the proposed subject and diagrams that it /^{10} was suggested should be used in the in-house magazine. /^{20} (**20**)

Exercise 13.3

There are many well-photographed advertisements that are aimed at /[10] children and warn of the dangers of speaking to strangers. /[20] **(20)**

Exercise 13.4

My main objection to geography at college is that I /[10] do not like the subject. Although I quite enjoy drawing /[20] diagrams and graphs, the rest of the lesson gives me /[30] a strange feeling. Perhaps I am prejudiced, but I wish /[40] I could reject it completely and exchange it instead for /[50] something much more interesting such as computer programming or photography. /[60] **(60)**

1 A memo to reception

I feel it would be a good idea to have /[10] some details handy at the front desk for people who /[20] are interested in Listed Buildings, Time Sharing, buying property abroad /[30] etc., as we are constantly being asked about these.

Ask /[40] Pauline if she can find some spare space in the /[50] display stand just inside the main door.

I jotted a /[60] few notes down as a starter whilst in the train /[70] which should be useful and will expand them tomorrow when /[80] I have more time. I am dashing off to a /[90] meeting right now and will be absent for the rest /[100] of the day. **(103)**

2 An article to be produced as a leaflet about living in Florida

Why don't you think about buying a house or business /[10] in Florida? Many people have already done so and many /[20] more are in the process of doing so.

If you /[30] don't know where to start, are wondering who offers the /[40] widest selection of properties, are doubtful of the best places /[50] to live, I can tell you categorically that your problem /[60] is settled. We are the local agents for the London /[70] based organisation dealing specifically with all types of property in /[80] the USA.

Florida offers a splendid lifestyle with /[90] warm weather all the year round, and the wide open /[100] spaces with very few people offer good opportunities for recreation. /[110]

There are no language barriers such as you may find /[120] in Europe, enabling you to take advantage of the social /[130] life of the district. A wide choice of homes and /[140] businesses is available in all regions and you can take /[150] your pick from sea front, lake side, river bank or /[160] even a town in the interior. Both houses and apartments /[170] are in great demand, but the expertise of the staff /[180] in London will help you to choose what is best /[190] for you at the price you are able to afford. /[200]

They will also arrange inspection trips to Florida with agents /[210] on hand to

enable prospective buyers to view and become /²²⁰ acquainted with the sites at first hand.
Ask here for /²³⁰ more information. (**232**)

3 An article about time share to be produced as a leaflet entitled 'The Pros and Cons of Time Share'

Time sharing enables the concept of owning a holiday home, /¹⁰ whether in this country or abroad, to become a reality. /²⁰ Time shares can be bought in country houses, converted castles, /³⁰ purpose built developments, flats and even boats.
What does time /⁴⁰ sharing mean? Well, it gives the buyer the right to /⁵⁰ spend a specific week or weeks each year in the /⁶⁰ chosen development. If the time share is freehold, the property /⁷⁰ could be yours for ever, but many people lease property /⁸⁰ for periods of, say, twenty or thirty years depending on /⁹⁰ circumstances. The cost varies according to the size of the /¹⁰⁰ development, the time of year, and is naturally more expensive /¹¹⁰ in the high season and during school holidays. Time sharing /¹²⁰ started in France during the late 1950s, quickly becoming /¹³⁰ popular in Europe and North America and later on in /¹⁴⁰ Britain with several nation-wide major developers taking the plunge /¹⁵⁰ and investing money.
On the debit side, a word of /¹⁶⁰ caution is necessary for would-be owners. First of all, /¹⁷⁰ you must be sure you wish to go to the /¹⁸⁰ same place year after year for a holiday. It might /¹⁹⁰ seem attractive for those with young families, but will teenagers /²⁰⁰ seek different, more adventurous, holidays as time passes? Although it /²¹⁰ is possible to exchange properties with other time sharers, this /²²⁰ can turn out to be a bit of a nuisance /²³⁰ and will have to be done through a specialised agency, /²⁴⁰ who will make quite a hefty charge for the privilege. /²⁵⁰
Another matter often overlooked is the management charge to cover /²⁶⁰ the cost of administration together with more practical details such /²⁷⁰ as maintenance, decoration and cleaning, which will probably rise every /²⁸⁰ year as the cost of living increases.
In times of /²⁹⁰ recession it might be difficult to re-sell your time /³⁰⁰ share once your enthusiasm has waned, so it certainly must /³¹⁰ not be seen as an investment or a quick way /³²⁰ of making a profit.
Time sharing must be put into /³³⁰ perspective. On the one hand, one hears strange stories, particularly /³⁴⁰ from abroad, but on the other hand many people enjoy /³⁵⁰ time sharing. If you think it may be the holiday /³⁶⁰ life for you, then go ahead, but take care not /³⁷⁰ to enter into any agreement without legal advice.
I must /³⁸⁰ point out that this Agency does not deal in time /³⁹⁰ share development either at home or abroad. This brief informatory /⁴⁰⁰ leaflet is

produced as a service to those clients who /⁴¹⁰ have expressed an interest. **(414)**

4 An article to be produced as a leaflet entitled 'Listed Buildings'. Roman numerals should be used for the four numbered points

Buildings are listed to ensure their preservation by the Department /¹⁰ of the Environment. Once a building is listed, legal protection /²⁰ is provided. Buildings fall into four main categories:

(i) Buildings /³⁰ built before 1700 which still survive in an almost /⁴⁰ original state.

(ii) Most buildings built between 1700 and /⁵⁰1840.

(iii) Buildings built between 1840 and 19 /⁶⁰14 which are quality buildings and the main work of /⁷⁰ principal architects.

(iv) Selected high quality buildings from 1914 /⁸⁰ to 1939.

The buildings chosen to be listed /⁹⁰ reflect their special architectural or planning value or their importance /¹⁰⁰ in illustrating social and economic history. **(106)**

Exercise 14.1

Exercise 14.2

The union <u>convened</u> a meeting in <u>Canterbury</u> yesterday afternoon to /¹⁰ discuss the as yet <u>unconfirmed</u> rumour that the company was /²⁰ to close due to this management. In the current <u>economic</u> /³⁰ climate it was <u>considered</u> unlikely that members would secure new /⁴⁰ jobs and it decided on a strong <u>campaign</u> to force /⁵⁰ management to <u>confirm</u> or deny the news before <u>continuing</u> with /⁶⁰ an alternative <u>scheme</u> for the <u>common</u> good of its members. /⁷⁰ **(70)**

Exercise 14.3

1 I <u>instinctively</u> know when I am about to <u>clinch</u> a profitable business deal <u>such</u> as the one I did yesterday afternoon, although I have no <u>inclination</u> to become a millionaire. **(30)**

2 The <u>enclosure</u> with this letter states that the total cost to <u>insulate</u> your loft in this <u>instance</u> <u>includes</u> VAT at the current rate. **(25)**

Exercise 14.4

We all live in a technological age and everyone is /[10] affected by it. We may not have the technical ability /[20] to understand the electronics industry or how atomic power is /[30] produced, but most of us can use a computer program /[40] on a microcomputer to calculate the circumference of a circle. /[50] **(50)**

Exercise 14.5

At a recent conference, a member of the local council /[10] congratulated our company on the thorough and comprehensive technical training /[20] of our staff as compared with our competitors. He stated /[30] that we were an inspiration to other commercial concerns in /[40] the local community. The councillor explained that in a recent /[50] telephone conversation with our MP at the House of /[60] Commons he discussed the importance of education and agreed that /[70] we must circumvent the mistaken belief that language skills are /[80] not as important as technical skills. **(86)**

1 Letter to a new retail customer

Dear Miss Wong

Thank you for your fax order for /[10] our comprehensive range of beauty products. I am pleased to /[20] welcome you as one of our new retail customers this /[30] season and hope that you will find our service and /[40] delivery efficient and speedy.

Your account number is 10 /[50]92849 and we would appreciate it /[60] if you would quote this number on all correspondence as /[70] it will expedite packing and delivery. A supply of our /[80] printed order forms is enclosed with this letter which will /[90] simplify your ordering procedure. You may use these forms to /[100] fax your order if you wish.

From time to time /[110] we have special offers for our retail customers and next /[120] month we will be promoting our range of cleansing milks /[130] and creams. For every fifty of each type ordered, you /[140] will receive five free. This means that you can put /[150] on a special promotion of your own to attract customers /[160] to buy our product, or perhaps give them away as /[170] free gifts.

I am enclosing some details of an exciting /[180] new competition for anyone who purchases any of our products. /[190] The prize is a superb two-week holiday for four /[200] people in Bermuda, and we expect our sales to increase /[210] immediately, particularly from existing customers, but we hope to tempt /[220] and encourage many new customers as well. The result of /[230] the competition will be announced at the end of March. /[240]

Our display pack will have already reached you and the /[250] ordered goods should arrive within the next couple of days. /[260]

Let me remind you of the importance of stressing that /[270] our products are made from pure vegetable ingredients, they are /[280] not tested on animals, and our packaging is produced from /²⁹⁰ 100 per cent recycled paper. Many people say they /³⁰⁰ buy our beauty products especially for this reason. Good luck /³¹⁰ with future sales.

Yours sincerely
Sales Manager
Four Seasons Beauty /³²⁰ (320)

2 Letter to a customer confirming a competition win

Dear Ms Cannon
This letter is to confirm our telephone /¹⁰ conversation of this morning when I informed you that you /²⁰ are the outright winner of the Four Seasons Beauty competition. /³⁰ Let me congratulate you. Your slogan was chosen as being /⁴⁰ the most appropriate by our panel of celebrity judges when /⁵⁰ compared with all the hundreds of other entries.
The superb /⁶⁰ prize, as you know, is an all-expenses-paid two- /⁷⁰week holiday in Bermuda for you and your family, flying /⁸⁰ first-class from Heathrow Airport. You may choose when you /⁹⁰ wish to go, to fit in with your annual holiday /¹⁰⁰ between now and the end of the year. You have /¹¹⁰ also won a complete range of Four Seasons Beauty products /¹²⁰ and a clothes voucher for £500 to be /¹³⁰ spent at a famous London store.
We would like you /¹⁴⁰ to be guest of honour at the award ceremony to /¹⁵⁰ be held on 15 March in the Conference Suite of /¹⁶⁰ the Beauty Trade Council building which is about five minutes' /¹⁷⁰ walk from the House of Commons. However, you will not /¹⁸⁰ be walking as we are providing a chauffeured limousine to /¹⁹⁰ transport you and your family from your home to the /²⁰⁰ venue and back home again after the event.
Before the /²¹⁰ reception our beauty specialists will style your hair and prepare /²²⁰ your make-up, and a leading designer is presenting you /²³⁰ with one of his dresses for you to wear at /²⁴⁰ the reception.
Jenny Spencer, the well-known beauty consultant and /²⁵⁰ counsellor, is to award the prizes and we expect press /²⁶⁰ and television reporters, as well as our own photographer, to /²⁷⁰ be there to record the event.
I will be in /²⁸⁰ touch with you again soon to finalise the details. Again, /²⁹⁰ many congratulations.

Yours sincerely
Mary Ellis
Sales Manager
Four Seasons /³⁰⁰ Beauty (301)

3 Letter to Miss Wong, a retail customer

Dear Miss Wong
You will be pleased to know that /¹⁰ one of your customers, Ms Cannon, has won our holiday /²⁰ competition. We would, therefore, like to invite you to

the $/^{30}$ award ceremony, details attached, where you yourself will receive a $/^{40}$ prize for being the retailer who sold our products to $/^{50}$ the competition winner. I do hope you can attend, and $/^{60}$ I shall be pleased to pay your travelling expenses from $/^{70}$ Canterbury to London.
I look forward to hearing from you. $/^{80}$
Yours sincerely **(82)**

Exercise 15.1

The <u>official</u> <u>documentation</u> with regard to entering for the <u>championship</u> $/^{10}$ is much too detailed. As this event is only held $/^{20}$ every two years, <u>specialised</u> printed forms are hardly <u>essential</u> and $/^{30}$ money is wasted which could be used more <u>efficiently</u> by $/^{40}$ the charities who are to benefit. In <u>addition</u>, it wastes $/^{50}$ the time of entrants who see this form filling as $/^{60}$ an <u>additional</u> <u>imposition</u> on their goodwill. A <u>conventional</u> A4 $/^{70}$ sheet setting out the <u>conditions</u>, with a <u>section</u> to be $/^{80}$ signed by the entrants and later <u>initialled</u> by the organisers, $/^{90}$ is surely <u>sufficient</u> and would cause no <u>hardship</u> to anyone. $/^{100}$ **(100)**

Exercise 15.2

(a) Good shorthand, typewriting and word processing qualifications are essential when $/^{10}$ applying for any sort of <u>situation</u> in the office world. $/^{20}$ Making sure there is no <u>inattention</u> on your part during $/^{30}$ lesson <u>sessions</u> should get you off to a significant start. $/^{40}$ **(40)**

(b) This <u>season</u> has seen a <u>substantial</u> increase in the wild $/^{10}$ bird <u>population</u> that has migrated to this part of the $/^{20}$ world. <u>Substantial</u> numbers of them have gathered and nested in $/^{30}$ wooded areas near the <u>railway station</u>. This school is <u>unofficially</u> $/^{40}$ recording <u>sufficient</u> <u>information</u> to enable us to identify the colony. $/^{50}$ **(50)**

1 Circular letter

Dear Sir or Madam
I hope you enjoyed your visit $/^{10}$ to the Leisure Exhibition held recently at the Conference Centre $/^{20}$ and possibly visited our stand whilst you were there. My $/^{30}$ reason for writing is that in this modern technological world $/^{40}$ which produces so much junk mail, I thought it appropriate $/^{50}$ to write and ask if you would like to be $/^{60}$ included on our mailing list as someone interested in making $/^{70}$ the most of your garden area during your leisure time. $/^{80}$ To keep you in the picture we would send you $/^{90}$ our Newsletter from time to time full of useful and $/^{100}$ helpful information and giving details of any special offers available. $/^{110}$
If you do not reply I can promise you that $/^{120}$ you will not be contacted again, but if you would $/^{130}$ like to receive our Newsletter simply complete the

address form /[140] attached and send it back to us in the pre- /[150]paid envelope.
I look forward to hearing from you.
Yours /[160] faithfully
Robert Eastwood (163)

WOLVERHAMPTON COLLEGE

2 Letter from Barbara Sadler asking for information

Dear Mr Eastwood
In reply to your letter of 15 /[10] February I was very pleased to hear that you produce /[20] a Newsletter. As I am an enthusiastic gardener, I would /[30] like to be included on your mailing list.
I did, /[40] indeed, visit your stand and spent some time looking at /[50] the diagrams of modern, relatively condensation-free conservatories. I also /[60] noticed you had a rather eye-catching, colourful leaflet on /[70] the History of Conservatories and would appreciate having a copy /[80] as, although I intended to collect one, my attention was /[90] distracted and I realised afterwards I had come away without /[100] one. Would it be possible for you to post one /[110] to me, please, when you send the Newsletter?
My present /[120] conservatory has been in existence since the house was built /[130] some fifty years ago, and as such is almost a /[140] museum piece, and probably due for replacement as it is /[150] far from being weatherproof.
I shall also be glad to /[160] see any catalogues you may have dealing with house extensions, /[170] conservatories, etc.
Yours sincerely
Barbara Sadler (176)

3 Letter of reply from Robert Eastwood, Managing Director

Dear Miss Sadler
Thank you for your letter of 2 /[10]1 February and interest in our goods. Unfortunately, we have /[20] no leaflets left on 'The Rise of the Conservatory' which /[30] I feel sure is the brochure you mean, as these /[40] were printed purely for the exhibition. However, I am enclosing /[50] a brief summary of its contents together with our catalogue /[60] and up-to-date price list. The prices stated will /[70] hold until the end of the year.
As your present /[80] conservatory is showing the effects of time and wear, I /[90] think you would enjoy looking round our display site where /[100] a wide range of conservatories, lean-to, free standing and /[110] to suit all sites and pockets, can be viewed. Three /[120] of our structures have been highly commended at national level /[130] this season and have won Approval Awards for design. Perhaps /[140] you could give me a ring on the Freefone number /[150] shown above and make an appointment to look round. I /[160] will then arrange for one

of my assistants to be /[170] on hand to deal with any enquiries you may have. /[180]

We also offer a dismantling and erecting service if desired, /[190] and will dispose of the old structure for you and /[200] also lay a new base if needed. Modern conservatories are /[210] designed to last, if not quite a lifetime, certainly for /[220] many years and represent excellent value for money. We are /[230] an old established firm and therefore pride ourselves on being /[240] able to supply a conservatory to suit everyone's needs.

Once /[250] again, thank you for your interest.

Yours sincerely

Robert Eastwood /[260]

Managing Director (**262**)

4 An article to accompany the previous letter

The Conservatory

The conservatory was, by and large, a Victorian /[10] development, although the Victorians were not responsible for starting the /[20] trend.

The first conservatories appeared in Italy where the first /[30] botanical gardens in the world made their appearance in the /[40] seventeenth century. They were far removed from our ideas of /[50] conservatories, having only small windows and little natural light. In /[60] the second half of the eighteenth century gardens of Royal /[70] palaces and stately homes all had their orangeries which acted /[80] as hothouses for citrus fruits and exotic plants. By the /[90] end of the century, heating systems and glass for windows /[100] had greatly improved and the nobility loved to impress their /[110] guests with brightly coloured tropical birds and out of season /[120] plants. By the mid nineteenth century the aim of middle- /[130]class Victorians was to have a conservatory which served as /[140] an entertainment and walking area with potted palms and greenery. /[150] During the last ten years the conservatory has had a /[160] great revival in popularity and families enjoy a larger living /[170] space and are able to extend the late summer and /[180] autumn months in an ultra modern, double glazed heated extension /[190] to the house. (**193**)

Exercise 15.3

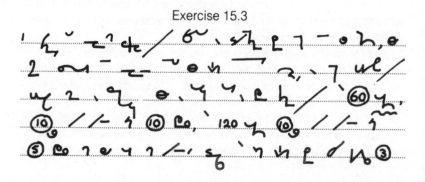

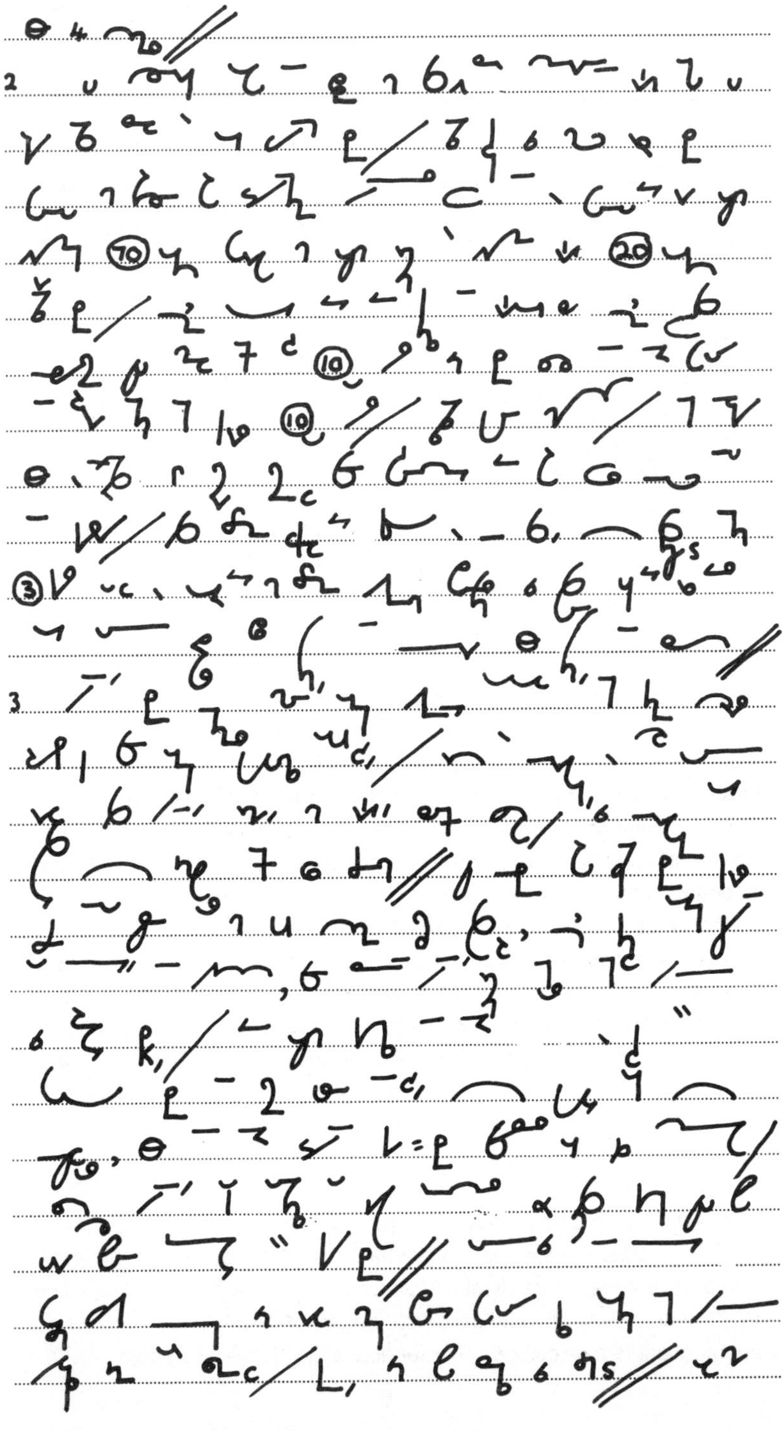

Exercise 16.1

For my business I need to know how many people /[10] can assemble in a small hall. There were 500 /[20] in the local community hall recently, but some larger halls /[30] hold 5000 people. I know that very large stadiums /[40] hold 100 000. If you go to a small /[50] amateur theatre production I can sell you the tickets for /[60] only a few pounds. On the other hand, a good /[70] ticket for a West End musical or an opera may /[80] cost you between £50 and £200. Thousands /[90] of people each day and millions of people each year /[100] go to the theatre on special occasions. Since the beginning /[110] of the century billions of people have been to the /[120] theatre and several billions of pounds have been spent on /[130] tickets all over the world, and I wish they had /[140] all bought their tickets from me! (146)

Exercise 16.2

My colleague goes abroad several times a year on business. /[10] Just before Easter she visited France and brought back 20 /[20] bottles of dry wine and some famous perfume for clients /[30] which cost her 500 francs. In the summer she /[40] went to Germany and bought 20 bottles of sweet wine /[50] for customers and a new company car for herself. I /[60] think she spent

80 000 DM. She has just come /⁷⁰ back from visiting the parent company in America and she /⁸⁰ bought lots of new items for the company which cost /⁹⁰ her 1000 dollars. **(94)**

Exercise 16.3

When you go to a different country on business you /¹⁰ have the difficulty of working out how much things cost. /²⁰ For example, what would 100 yen buy in Japan, /³⁰ 2000 lire in Italy, 25 francs in Belgium, /⁴⁰ or 300 pesetas in Spain? If you go to /⁵⁰ just one country you soon get used to the currency, /⁶⁰ but if you are touring round Europe it is more /⁷⁰ difficult. It is a good thing that measurements do not /⁸⁰ vary (dash) 4 kilometres, 3 kilograms and 5 litres are /⁹⁰ the same whether you are in France, Germany, Spain or /¹⁰⁰ Italy. **(101)**

Exercise 16.4

1 The Annual General Meeting of the Woodhouse School Parent Teachers' Association was held last night. **(15)**
2 PAYE is generally deducted from the salary of every employee who works for the NHS. **(20)**
3 If you buy any goods for the business office from the DIY store do be sure to obtain a VAT receipt. **(25)**
4 The applicant for this situation has 5 GCSEs, NVQ level 2 in Business Administration, and RSA certificates in typewriting, shorthand, and word processing. **(30)**
5 Our interest rate on all outstanding credit is 25 per cent per annum whilst our EC competitors' rate is 2 per cent higher at 27 per cent. **(30)**

1 Letter offering a mortgage to a customer

Dear Ms Dixon

I am pleased to be able to /¹⁰ inform you that your mortgage application made on 17 May /²⁰ to this bank for £50 000 in respect of /³⁰ the 2-bedroomed property known as Rose Cottage, 27 /⁴⁰ Mill Lane, Cambridge, has been approved, subject to improvements being /⁵⁰ made as outlined in the survey. The endowment mortgage with /⁶⁰ profits which you requested has a 25 year term. /⁷⁰ The current rate of interest is 11.5 per /⁸⁰ cent and the interest of £44/⁹⁰2 is payable monthly direct to the bank, whilst the /¹⁰⁰ premium of £60.57 on the endowment /¹¹⁰ is payable to the insurance company you have appointed. You /¹²⁰ also elected to include the house contents insurance with your /¹³⁰ mortgage payments at an extra cost of £300 /¹⁴⁰ per annum.

I must advise you at this time, however, /¹⁵⁰ that if for any reason you default on your payments, /¹⁶⁰ your home is at risk. Therefore, if at any time /¹⁷⁰ in the future you are in unexpected financial difficulties, please /¹⁸⁰ inform us immediately.

I wish you every happiness in your /¹⁹⁰ new home.

Yours sincerely

Andrew Sutton

Manager **(197)**

2 Letter to customers about credit card charges

Dear Customer

With effect from 4 September a standard annual /¹⁰ fee of £12 will be introduced for credit cardholders. /²⁰ This will be debited to your account on the day /³⁰ of the first card transaction after this date. This enables /⁴⁰ us to reduce the interest rate from 29. /⁵⁰8 per cent APR for purchases and 30 /⁶⁰.3 per cent APR for cash advances /⁷⁰ to 26.5 per cent and 28 /⁸⁰ per cent respectively. The APR for cash advance /⁹⁰ includes a handling charge of 1.5 per cent. /¹⁰⁰ Within 25 days of the statement date the cardholder /¹¹⁰ must pay 5 per cent or £10, whichever is /¹²⁰ the greater.

Remember that if you pay for public transport /¹³⁰ or car hire you are still automatically covered for travel /¹⁴⁰ insurance up to £50 000. Also, goods purchased with /¹⁵⁰ our credit card are insured for a period of twenty- /¹⁶⁰ eight days against loss or accident.

If your card is /¹⁷⁰ lost, stolen or misused without your consent, you should telephone /¹⁸⁰ our hotline on 0223 384 /¹⁹⁰39 and confirm in writing within 7 days. However, /²⁰⁰ you may be liable for the first £25 /²¹⁰ of any loss. Enclosed is your new credit agreement.

Yours /²²⁰ sincerely **(221)**

3 Letter to customers about savings schemes for children

Dear Customer

We all realise the value of saving for /¹⁰ the future and how important it is to save for /²⁰ a good education or just a rainy day. You may /³⁰ have children or grandchildren of your own and wish to /⁴⁰ set aside some money on a regular basis for their /⁵⁰ future. We have two different types of account to offer /⁶⁰ you.

Firstly, the Young Savers Plan which pays 8. /⁷⁰5 per cent interest. You may open this account with /⁸⁰ as little as £5 and add to it regularly, /⁹⁰ for example through a standing order 12 times a year. /¹⁰⁰ Up to £100 may be withdrawn instantly at /¹¹⁰ any of our branches with no loss of interest.

Secondly, /¹²⁰ if you have a larger sum to invest on behalf /¹³⁰ of a child, the Young Investors Plan is ideal for /¹⁴⁰ you. The minimum investment is £200, but there /¹⁵⁰ is a guaranteed higher interest rate of 10 per cent /¹⁶⁰ on this account, although there would be a loss of /¹⁷⁰ interest if sums of money are withdrawn without notice. When /[180] either of these accounts is opened we provide 2 free /[190] gifts: a piggy bank to encourage the child to save, /[200] and a personalised folder in which to keep statements.

Any /[210] child under the age of 16 who is not a /[220] taxpayer may receive gross interest on any account held in /[230] their name or on their behalf. There is a financial /[240] adviser at the above branch who would be pleased to /[250] give you more details.

Yours faithfully
Andrew Sutton
Manager (**259**)

4 Letter to customer about foreign currency

Dear Mr Patel
I am pleased to inform you that /[10] the foreign currency you ordered for your business trip, i /[20]e (colon)

30 000 yen
30 000 lire
400 /[30] Belgian francs and
1500 pesetas

together with £5/[40]00 of travellers' cheques, is awaiting collection. Yours sincerely (**49**)

Appendix 1
Special outlines

Listed alphabetically

	Unit		Unit
absolute/ly	8	fire	10
access	12	frequent	10
advantage	4	husband	1
after	6	identification	6
agriculture	5	identify	6
appropriate	5	importance	14
approval	5	improve/ment	5
because	12	inability	8
category	4	inattention	15
commercial	14	inch/es	6
community	14	inexperience	10
comprehensive	14	inform/ation	15
conference	4	insignificant	6
congratulate	5	insuperable	8
congratulations	5	major	13
council	14	motorway	11
councillor/counsellor	14	multiple	10
disadvantage	9	newspaper	1
employment	10	obvious	6
enclosure/s	1	perfect/ly	4
England	9	population	15
English	9	prefer	5
evidence	9	prejudice	13
exchange	10	preliminary	5
extra	4	probable	5

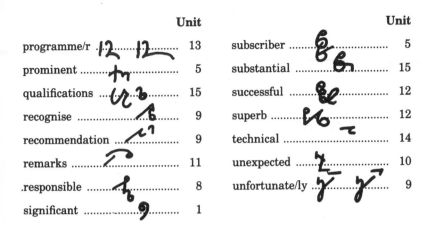

	Unit		Unit
programme/r	13	subscriber	5
prominent	5	substantial	15
qualifications	15	successful	12
recognise	9	superb	12
recommendation	9	technical	14
remarks	11	unexpected	10
responsible	8	unfortunate/ly	9
significant	1		

Appendix 2
Distinguishing outlines

Listed alphabetically

	Unit		Unit
explosion	10	expulsion	10
extract	10	extricate	10
industries	9	industrious	9
in fact	3	in effect	3
man	6	men	6
nine	6	noon	6
personal	1	personnel	1
psychology	8	sociology	8
season	15	session	15
station	15	situation	15
to do	9	today	9
woman	6	women	6

Appendix 3
Word groupings

Listed alphabetically

	Unit
after all	6
after that	6
all things being equal	8
almost impossible	8
Annual General Meeting	16
as a matter of course	11
as far as	10
at a	6
at the present time	5
at your earliest convenience	7
audio-visual	6
best of luck	11
between the	9
Board of Directors	4
by all means	11
by and large	11
change of address	7
down the	9
first of all	10
for ever and ever	10
from time to time	4
House of Commons	14
I look forward	2
if this is the	12
in reply to your letter	7

	Unit
it was a	6
it was an	6
Ladies and Gentlemen	11
large number of	7
Managing Director	4
member of staff	11
members of staff	11
Mr and Mrs	11
multi-storey car park	11
out of stock	7
prompt attention	7
regret to inform you	7
shopping precinct	5
take this opportunity	7
telephone conversation	14
that this is	12
this is	12
this is the	12
unable to obtain	7
we have received your letter	7
we were sorry	7
weeks ago	8
word processing	5
years ago	8
years of age	8